brilliant

numeracy
tests

brilliant

numeracy
tests

Robert Williams

Prentice Hall
is an imprint of

Harlow, England • London • New York • Boston • San Francisco • Toronto • Sydney • Singapore • Hong Kong
Tokyo • Seoul • Taipei • New Delhi • Cape Town • Madrid • Mexico City • Amsterdam • Munich • Paris • Milan

PEARSON EDUCATION LIMITED

Edinburgh Gate
Harlow CM20 2JE
Tel: +44 (0)1279 623623
Fax: +44 (0)1279 431059
Website: www.pearsoned.co.uk

First published in Great Britain in 2010

© Pearson Education Limited 2010

The right of Robert Williams to be identified as author of this work has been
asserted by him in accordance with the Copyright, Designs and Patents Act
1988.

ISBN: 978-0-273-72465-0

British Library Cataloguing-in-Publication Data
A catalogue record for this book is available from the British Library

Library of Congress Cataloging-in-Publication Data
A catalog record for this book is available from the Library of Congress

10 9 8 7 6 5 4 3 2 1
14 13 12 11 10

Typeset in 10/14pt Plantin by 3
Printed in Great Britain by Henry Ling Ltd., at the Dorset Press, Dorchester,
Dorset

The publisher's policy is to use paper manufactured from sustainable forests.

For my inspirational daughters, Eve and Rose, and my indispensable parents, Richard and Marion Williams.

Contents

About the author

Rob Williams is a chartered occupational psychologist with over twelve years' experience in the design and delivery of ability tests. Having worked for several of the UK's leading test publishers, he has written many numeracy tests and presented his research at home and abroad. Today he heads up Rob Williams Assessment Ltd, an independent company specialising in assessment for recruitment. Rob has run hundreds of assessment centres for numerous public sector organisations and private companies – giving him valuable insight into how testing is used in a wide range of businesses. When he's not working, Rob enjoys spending time with his two young daughters, going to the cinema and playing tennis.

To find out more see www.robwilliamsassessment.co.uk

Acknowledgements

I would like to thank the following people for their help in this book's practice questions: Anne Marie Ryan, Helene Ryan, Gabby Evans and my parents.

While every effort has been taken to ensure that the practice questions in this book accurately replicate the actual tests, test formats do change periodically. It is therefore wise to always consult your testing organization's website for the most up-to-date information about your test.

Foreword

Numeracy tests are amongst the most widespread measures that employers apply in selecting staff. I have come across their use for shop-floor factory and retail staff, for computer programmers, croupiers, sales people, managers, space scientists and top civil servants. The last group included the head of the Inland Revenue – the most senior tax job in the country – and it was interesting that even there not all of the highly qualified candidates did well! So, numeracy tests are widely valued by employers to help them make distinctions amongst candidates who might otherwise seem to be much of a muchness. I have also become aware that facing a numeracy test is a big challenge for many. It is more often with this type of test than any other that the 'rabbit in the headlights' reaction is found; some people are just too alarmed to demonstrate their true numerical ability. And then there are those who have a blind spot in one or more areas of working with numbers, perhaps going back many years so that decimals or percentages, say, always floor them.

This book is for all those who can anticipate taking numerical reasoning tests, but who know that they might not do themselves justice – and that is a very large group. It is not only the fearful or those with the blind spots, but also those who are rusty with numbers, perhaps not having had to use them much in their work for several years. The emphasis of the book is on practice and it is a particularly rich source of sample material of all types of numerical reasoning items that gives readers the opportunity for a dedicated course of exercise to improve their performance. In addition to the sample tests there are a host of tips to ensure that the right approach to practice is adopted, such as examining what might lead you to have guessed an answer and how each bit of practice can be seen as like a single coin – 'not worth much on its own, but valuable when you amass several, giving you a wealth of knowledge'.

Whilst stressing the use of the practice material as such, the book also advises on how to make use of day-to-day opportunities to hone numerical skills, from splitting a restaurant bill, to tracking darts scores. Altogether this is a very comprehensive and rounded volume for anyone seriously wishing to do brilliantly at numerical reasoning tests.

Dr Robert Edenborough
Director, Bradenlaw Ltd

PART 1

Getting to grips with your test

Was the last time you did maths at school? Let me guess – was it your least favourite subject? Does the thought of being tested on your numeracy skills strike fear in your heart? If so, don't worry – many people share your anxiety. But remember: anyone can improve!

You should not underestimate the competition you are facing from other test-takers, but if you are prepared to work hard you can put up a good challenge. Try approaching your upcoming numeracy test like a running race. You would not just turn up at the starting line and hope for the best, would you? Instead, you would go out for training runs in the preceding weeks – starting with easy jogs then building up to faster sprints. On the race day you would want to be rested, relaxed, and in peak physical and mental condition. This book coaches you to prepare for your numeracy test in a similar way – by providing ample practice opportunities and strategies to use on your test day. You are not striving for a gold medal here, but success on a numeracy test may be a stepping stone to a new job, a promotion or a place on a degree course.

Whether you are a beginner or an experienced test-taker you can benefit from more practice. This book can help you in three main ways:

1 *Developing your test-taking strategy*
   You may want to read through this book for general advice

on test-taking. Equally, you may want to flick through and highlight the individual tips most relevant to you.

2   *Targeted practice with a specific test format*
To maximise your improvement, you need to practise with questions that are similar in format and difficulty level to your actual test. The practice questions in this book mirror the specific format of many common tests. If you will be taking one of these featured tests, you should start your preparation with the most-relevant practice questions.

3   *Improving the speed with which you answer questions*
If, after doing targeted practice, you are still motivated to improve, you can tackle subsequent sections of slightly harder questions. This extra practice should improve the speed with which you answer easier questions.

CHAPTER 1

What are numeracy tests?

Ability tests, such as numeracy tests, are designed to measure specific abilities relevant for success in a particular course, profession or job. Sometimes these tests are referred to as psychometric or aptitude tests. Numeracy tests are an objective and accurate means of assessing a candidate's potential effectiveness whenever there is a numerical component to a particular job role or course.

What do numeracy tests measure?

In simple terms a numeracy test is a means of assessing a person's ability to work with numerical information. They provide an objective measure of many numerical reasoning abilities, including the following:

> a numeracy test is a means of assessing a person's ability to work with numerical information

- interpreting statistical data;
- analysing complex mathematical information presented in graphs, pie-charts, tables, etc.;
- solving problems that require an understanding of basic mathematical operations (e.g. fractions, ratios, percentages);
- using and interpreting financial information correctly.

Most numeracy tests are multiple choice. They can be offered in either a traditional pen-and-paper format or online. Needless to say you cannot buy these tests in advance of sitting them – so it is essential that you prepare thoroughly.

> ### ☀ **brilliant** tip
>
> Calculators are allowed so ensure that you know how to use one effectively. It is important for you to be able to input complex calculations quickly.

Why do I have to take a numeracy test?

The modern world's recruitment and selection processes are increasingly sophisticated. Many medium-sized and large employers now make extensive use of ability tests as part of their standard recruitment processes. Numeracy tests are also increasingly part of the entry requirements for certain professions and postgraduate degree courses.

> many medium-sized and large employers now make extensive use of ability tests

Ability tests allow employers and university admissions offices to assess a large number of applicants for competitive positions in a standardised way. In other words the same ability test can be given to a large number of applicants and the standardised results used as an efficient means of comparision.

There is another key attraction to using a standardised process rather than, for example, relying upon old-fashioned, unstructured interviews where every applicant would be asked different questions. Any selection process should be fair to all applicants and provide a clear picture of individual strengths and weaknesses in particular areas. Even if you do not like the idea of being tested on your numeracy skills at least you know that it is fair, since everyone has to do the same test!

The overall aim is for the best people to be selected – and the use of ability tests differentiates the high performers from the low performers. A numeracy test will sort out the better performers on mathematical ability. A well-designed numeracy test is a reliable and consistent means of assessing the numeracy skills required for effective work performance. The more difficult numeracy tests are suitable to use where a higher level of numerical ability is required to operate effectively in that working environment.

brilliant tip

There is a way to tip the scales in your favour. You can probably see this coming... practising and familiarising yourself with the right type of numeracy questions will give you an advantage.

You might be thinking, 'Why do I have to take a numeracy test? I don't want to be a mathematician!' But it is not just mathematicians – or even bankers – who need proficient numeracy skills. Many different jobs

> many different jobs require an ability to work confidently with numbers

require an ability to work confidently with numbers in order to carry out a range of responsibilities effectively. This could involve anything from interpreting production quotas to carrying out technical work that relies upon detailed calculations. Whereas an accountant will have demonstrated his or her numerical abilities in the process of acquiring a professional qualification, other career paths depend on numeracy tests to measure applicants' skill in this area. Even managers who are not going to be responsible for producing financial reports are still likely to be presented with a numeracy test at interview. This is because they would still be expected to understand any data that is presented as tables, graphs or charts.

Still not convinced? Let's look at a few jobs that involve more numeracy than you might expect.

Retail sales

Selling is not just about slick presentation skills and a flair for customer relations. At the entry level, retail sales jobs require the ability to handle money correctly and to deal with customers' transactions competently. Mistakes here could be very costly. At a more senior level, numeracy is used to analyse sales figures, produce account sheets and balance budgets.

Teacher

To teach numeracy, it makes sense that you would need first to be proficient yourself. But even if you do not wish to be a maths teacher, many other academic disciplines require dexterity with numbers. For example, all the sciences use mathematical calculations. Music, design, ITC: all of these fields involve an element of maths. Even home economics involves working with measurements. Teachers also need numerical abilities to calculate students' grades, to understand performance targets, and to comply with school and departmental budgets.

Manager

the placing of people in jobs should not be *solely* dependent on their numeracy test results

Managers need to be able to quickly and effectively digest figures and statistics for their team, department or region. They need to analyse profit and loss figures and to track their own budgets as part of this financial management process.

How hard will it be?

The numeracy test practice questions featured in this book span a wide range of difficulty levels. This is deliberate and reflects the range of tests in current usage. Starting with the easiest and getting increasingly difficult, the practice questions cover the full range of numerical reasoning ability.

The initial questions involve only the most basic mathematical operations – for example, how to use subtraction, addition, multiplication and division. These are followed by increasingly complex questions using ratios, decimal points, fractions and percentages. At the next level, the practice questions involve more complex features, such as the conversion of measurements between different systems (e.g. changing pounds sterling into another currency). The graduate-level practice questions require the interpretation of statistical data shown in charts and on graphs. The final numeracy practice questions, targeted at senior managers, involve the analysis of complex financial data.

Remember, you are not about to sit an A-level Maths test. Areas such as complex algebra and the use of mathematical formulae are not included in any of the practice questions. The more esoteric mathematical operations, such as powers, square roots, prime numbers and probabilities, will also be avoided as they rarely appear in numeracy tests.

> remember, you are not about to sit an A-level Maths test

Most of the test questions will be multiple choice. Don't be fooled into thinking this makes them easier. Having written many numeracy tests myself I can assure you that is not the case. The answer options are designed to be deliberately tricky and to catch out any sloppy errors. Remember: multiple choice does not mean multiple guess. If you want to pass, you need to be able to work out the answers.

> multiple choice does not mean multiple guess

↗ brilliant recap

- There's no getting away from it. Numeracy testing is now widely used in the application process for many jobs and courses.

- Well-designed numeracy tests are used because they predict future performance at work.

- Your numeracy test should mirror the maths calculations and problems that will occur in the role that you are applying for.

- There are many different types of numeracy test on the market, at varying levels of difficulty.

CHAPTER 2

Getting started

Right, let's get down to work. First think about how much time you can spare for practising. Then set aside the time so you can conduct as many reading and practice sessions as possible over a period of several weeks or months. This is preferable to reading through this book in two or three sittings.

You may like to set aside a particular time at the weekends, or at a time of day when your mind is most alert. Once you've committed to a practice session, make sure you stick to it.

> once you've committed to a practice session, make sure you stick to it

Go on – start practising as soon as you can!

Why should I practise?

Test-taking experience is known to significantly improve your chances of passing a numeracy test, so you need to squeeze in as much advance practice as possible. Make a commitment to practise as much as you can to improve your confidence and help you keep a clear head on the day. You'll find plenty of practice questions in Part 2.

The amount of time needed to raise your performance level will vary between a few hours of work for those who are just a little bit rusty to many days for others. Although less experienced readers will need to put in more work, they should also see the most dramatic improvement through practice. Popular tests share similar formats so there will be several test chapters that are useful for you to practice. You can get extra practice by completing those practice questions similar to your test.

Is practising enough?

If you don't already know exactly what type of numeracy test you will be taking, you should find out as your first step. That way you will know what type of questions you need to practise. You also need to know what to expect on the actual test day. This book provides all the background information that you need on your specific type of test and the testing process in general. Going into the test feeling knowledgeable should considerably reduce your anxiety.

going into the test feeling knowledgeable should reduce your anxiety

Why is this test so important?

Broadly speaking, the earlier in an assessment process that you are being asked to complete a numeracy test then the more important it is to pass. When a test is used to gain entry to a profession or course it is a sifting process. The test must be passed to progress – anyone who does not pass is sifted out. If you wish to join the armed forces, apply to medical school, or achieve Qualified Teacher Status you will need to pass a numeracy test.

You may have been informed that you will be taking a numeracy test as part of an assessment centre procedure. Here the test is one part of several assessments, which may include an interview, presentation, group exercise and a role play. You may also have to take other tests, such as a verbal reasoning test or a personality questionnaire. It is still important to pass, but in this case you are not being sifted on the basis of the numeracy test alone.

 **warning**

Even if your numeracy test is only one component of your assessment centre, don't get cavalier. You don't want a poor performance on the numeracy test to be the thing that holds you back.

If the numeracy test is only one part of that day's assessment remember to treat each assessment as a separate opportunity to show how you can perform under pressure. If you are unhappy with your performance on the numeracy test don't let it drag down your performance on any other area. Similarly, if you are disappointed with how you did on another assessment, make a fresh start with the numeracy test.

Practice stages

I suggest breaking down each practice session into three linked stages:

1 *Before* taking a practice test.

2 *During* the practice test.

3 *After* taking a practice test.

Before taking a practice test ...

- Plan which questions you are going to answer. Then you can get going straight away instead of wasting time flicking through the book.

- Identify a quiet place to work where you are unlikely to be disturbed.

- Set aside at least forty minutes to concentrate on working your way through a large number of the practice questions.

- Sit at a desk and before starting clear away anything that may distract you.

- Have scrap paper, pencils and a calculator nearby and ready for use.

- Turn your mobile phone off.

- Have a clock or watch handy to time how quickly you work.

During the practice test ...

- Treat it as a real test session to help you get into the right mindset. This will help reduce any nerves on the test day, even if that day will certainly be more stressful.

- Work systematically through all the questions in the relevant section. You need to attempt every question: do not cherry pick or randomly select questions. The reason for this is simple: you need to identify whether there are specific types of questions where your performance would benefit from further practice.

- Motivate yourself to answer each question as effectively as you can.

brilliant tip

If you finish earlier than you expected then – just as you would on the real test – use this extra time as an ideal opportunity to go back and double-check any questions that you were unsure about.

After taking a practice test ...

- Set aside a time for marking your test when you will be uninterrupted.

- Circle those answers which are incorrect.

- Go through each answer explanation for those questions that you got wrong.

It is really important to review your progress regularly. Reflect upon the way that you completed the tests – as well as your overall performance. Focus on how you can avoid making the same mistakes again. You need to

> it is really important to review your progress regularly

establish which part or parts of the calculation you carried out incorrectly. Try highlighting the answer explanations that you found most useful so you can review them again and again. If you do this just before your next practice session it will help engrain the correct way of working in your mind.

Progress review

When you review your performance, ask yourself the following questions:

- How many questions did I get right?
- How many questions did I get wrong?
- If this is not your first practice session – Have I improved? For which types of question?
- What have I learnt?
- Are there particular types of question that I get wrong?
- Is there one specific thing that the answer explanation taught me? Have I applied this learning point correctly the next time around?

brilliant tip

Do not be concerned if your preferred method differs from the explanation given. The key thing is to know how you can get at the correct answer when a similar question comes up.

It may be the last thing you want to do after taking the actual test, but on your test day you should also reflect on what – if any –

questions you struggled with. This will help you target areas to improve if you face another numeracy test.

I am having trouble getting started

Has your test preparation ground to a halt? Or maybe you haven't even managed to get started yet. Why not try a SWOT analysis to show how far you have come already and where you need to go? A SWOT analysis is a tool often used in business for strategic planning. This might sound intimidating, but it is really just a list. Four lists, in fact: **S**trengths; **W**eaknesses; **O**pportunities; **T**hreats. For example, the threat of failing the test if you don't start practising soon!

Here are a few other suggestions for a SWOT analysis:

Strengths:

- You've bought this book with the intention to read it and improve.

- Time is on your side – don't waste a second more – start practising right away.

Weaknesses:

- There is one section of the test that you are dreading. There you go – start your practice on that area of the test now.

- You know that you never got the hang of fractions or reading from complex graphs. Better focus your practice on precisely those questions.

Opportunities:

- Turn off the TV in the evening or at weekends. Then you can use that time to practise.

- Set aside your lunch break to practise, or get up half an hour earlier if you work best in the morning.

Threats:

- You don't spend enough time preparing in advance.

- You tend to procrastinate, or get easily distracted.
- You haven't kept up with your initial commitment to do as much preparation as possible.

Common concerns

If you are feeling apprehensive about your test take comfort in knowing that you are not alone – many people find the prospect of sitting a test quite daunting. Let's look at a few common concerns.

How do I know I am improving?

Effective feedback is the key to improving your overall performance. That means going through the answer explanations in detail. Try other practice sections or, after a period of time, attempt the same test questions again. This will allow you to gauge your improvement in performance over time.

- Have you learnt where your strengths and weaknesses are in terms of overall numerical reasoning abilities? Is it ratios, or percentages that you are still having trouble with? Once you are aware of where any weakness lies then it is important to focus future practice testing on this area.
- Be honest with yourself about how much time you need to commit for extra practice.
- Keep a record of how many questions you get right.

Here are some questions to ask yourself in order to raise your awareness of potential pitfalls.

Q Did you rush through the questions rather than working at a steady pace?

A Most tests are timed so you need to cultivate a focused and alert approach. Your first priority is to work accurately. There's no benefit in getting questions wrong. But don't take a leisurely approach, either. The guy sitting next to you may pass because he answered more questions than you – even though he also got more questions wrong.

Ⓠ Did you miss out any questions? If so did you make a note and go back to these at the end of your session?

Ⓐ This is a key test-taking strategy. It only works if you make sure to mark the question you omitted. You also need to work at such a pace that you have time to return to it at the end. Still, I can't recommend the strategy highly enough. We all encounter questions that we can't do, or just don't like the look of. If you find that you are spending longer than you would like on one question then make the judgement call and move on.

Ⓠ Did you spend too much time going over the question itself and the numerical information given at the start?

Ⓐ It is tempting to be over cautious. Did the question really say that? What were the units again? You need to cultivate a focused concentration that allows you to read the question, memorise what you're being asked to do and then know once you have the required answer.

brilliant tip

Remember that all questions are worth the same. No one cares if you leave a couple out. The important thing is to answer as many correctly as you can.

Where do I need to improve most?

It's vital to know where you need to improve most. Knowing this will help you to use your preparation time wisely – enabling you to tailor your practice sessions around the areas you most need to improve. Ask yourself the following questions to home in on any problem areas.

Q Is there a pattern emerging in what type of questions I get wrong?

A If a particular type of question recurs then it makes sense to spend additional time making sure that you are comfortable with these questions. Don't assume that you can pass without learning how to answer that sort of question.

Q Is there a pattern emerging in where I get questions wrong?

A If you make more mistakes near the start of your practice session then this could be a consequence of nerves and taking time to settle down. You need to work on focusing 100% as soon as you start the test. If you make more mistakes near the end of your practice session then this could be a result of losing concentration or rushing the last few questions. Practise pacing yourself. You need to learn to work steadily, and in a high state of mental alertness, throughout an entire test.

Q Were there particular types of numerical reasoning questions that I guessed?

A This may be a sign that you need to go back to basics. If you are guessing questions involving percentages then you need to learn the basics of how percentages work. Do this before attempting any more practice questions.

I'm not getting any better . . .

Are you sure? Don't be too hard on yourself – remember that your improvement will occur gradually, not after just one practice session. You'll only get better if you learn from your mistakes, though, so reflect upon the following questions.

> your improvement will occur gradually, not after just one practice session

ⓠ Am I clear on why I got each question wrong?

ⓐ You may like to write down or highlight where you went wrong so that the next time you practise you can remind yourself.

ⓠ Did I make far too many careless mistakes?

ⓐ This is a clear indication that you need to slow down your pace. Yes, you need to work briskly, but the key is to find an efficient pace that still allows you all the time that you need to get questions right.

Help! I don't have much time . . .

Ideally you will have sufficient time to plan your practice sessions over a period of several weeks. Many test-taking strategies take time to develop. For those readers who are less lucky and only have a matter of days then your first priority is to complete those practice questions most relevant to you in Part II. This will prepare you for what to expect, and improve your overall confidence.

Practice timetables

If you have 1 day . . .

- Read through the tactics and techniques in Chapter 4. Which of these appeal to you? Learn how to apply as many as you can in the time available before your test.

- Spend as much time as you can familiarising yourself with your test format, using the relevant chapter in Part 2.

If you have 1 week . . .

- Plan at least two practice sessions and start with the most relevant questions in Part 2. The chapters in Part 2 increase in difficulty level, so move backwards or forwards through Part 2 depending on whether you need to build your confidence with easier questions, or challenge yourself with tougher questions.

● In addition to the test-taking tactics in Chapter 4 there are tips and strategies spread out through all the chapters. Reading and applying these will help improve your overall speed and accuracy, so it is worth scanning every chapter for tips.

If you have 1 month . . .

● In addition to the above actions you have the luxury of scheduling in regular (at least bi-weekly) practice sessions over the course of the month, taking care to review and learn from the answer explanations.

● Each chapter in Part 2 also suggests additional sources of practice, such as online practice testing sites. If time permits, try taking these online practice tests.

If you are short of time then there are lots of other everyday opportunities to brush up on your application of simple mathematic operations (addition, subtraction, multiplication, division). These activities will improve your mental agility in tandem with working your way through the practice questions.

● When you are at the supermarket or shopping online try keeping a running tally in your head of the items that you intend to purchase. Even if it is only an approximate figure, check how close it is to the final total when you go to pay.

● When you dine at a restaurant use mental arithmetic to calculate what you should leave as a tip. Try working out the service charge at different percentages. If you are splitting the bill with friends, do the division in your head. When paying, quickly work out how much change you should receive.

● Your daily newspaper offers many great ways to sharpen your numeracy skills. Have a go at the mathematical puzzles, such as Sudoko. When looking at the weather report try switching the temperatures between Fahrenheit and Centigrade – how do these compare? Check out the previous day's share movements. Imagine if you had invested £1,000 in one of the shares listed. How much would you have gained or lost yesterday? When you see complex tables and graphs of statistical data don't move on to the next section. Spend time reviewing the axes of the graph and the headings of the table. Look at the title and the passage of text then ask yourself which points the figures are being used to illustrate. *The Financial Times* is a good source of this sort of material.

● Get hold of some business journals and/or company reports. Review the parts of these that contain a lot of figures. Can you work out the main themes shown by the data?

● Go through some of your old bank statements or telephone bills. Sum up the individual entries in as fast a time as possible by rounding up the decimal places.

● When you are playing – or watching – sports where there are high scores involved, such as darts and snooker, try to track the scores in your head.

> make the most of these everyday encounters to practise

You should definitely make the most of these everyday encounters to practise. But although beneficial, these activities are not as important as working through the practice questions in this book. Tackling the practice questions is by far the most effective way to improve your performance. If you want even more test-taking experience, other books and online sites offer additional practice material. And if you find that your mathematical skills are rustier than you'd like, an evening class in maths would be an ideal way to get help. Further education colleges routinely offer courses in numeracy skills.

⚡ brilliant do's and don'ts

DO

✓ Keep practising right up to the day before you are going to be taking your test.

✓ Study the format of the questions that you will be taking and focus your initial practice sessions on these questions.

✓ Continue practising with similar questions of a similar format. See if you are comfortable doing more difficult questions by going forwards in this book. Otherwise, attempt the preceding questions.

✓ Start by doing as many questions as you can in an untimed, informal session.

✓ Challenge yourself. Focus your efforts on understanding why you keep getting particular questions wrong and on avoiding any common mistakes.

✓ To gain further improvement, set a 30 minute time limit and complete as many of the questions in the relevant part as you can.

DON'T

✗ Only look once at where you went wrong. You'll probably have forgotten why in a few days' time. You should go back over your mistakes a few days later to ensure that what you have learned enters your long-term memory.

✗ Assume that the types of questions you struggle with won't come up in the test. Think of it a different way. Let's say that 1 in 10 of the test questions will be of a type that you have skipped over. That means that your maximum score is already 10% less than everyone else's ... and you haven't even started the test yet! Wouldn't you like to start with the same chance as those who are fully prepared?

✗ Think that you can just try harder on the test day and all will be OK. There's absolutely no getting away from it – preparation is crucial. Plus, you will have other stresses to contend with on the big day.

CHAPTER 3

Brush up your maths skills

Has it been a while since you used basic mental arithmetic? There are many mathematical rules that you learned when you were at school but you may since have forgotten. If your basic maths skills have become a little rusty then the following section can help you brush up. In order to pass your test, you will need to be able to perform calculations quickly and accurately in your head.

Are you panicking? If so, don't. Remember that somewhere, deep inside your mind, your maths knowledge is still there – you just need to brush away the cobwebs. As you work through the practice questions and the answer explanations, you should hopefully find these skills coming back to you. This book doesn't set out to re-teach the basics, but instead aims to improve the numeracy skills that you already possess. Let's start by ensuring that you have a clear understanding of the following basic maths skills:

> somewhere, deep inside your mind, your maths knowledge is still there

1 basic numerical operations;

2 the metric system of measurement;

3 more complex mathemetical operations.

If you are certain that you have these maths basics covered then you should skip ahead.

Basic numerical operations

Basic numerical reasoning requires an ability to manipulate numerical information in ways that you will have learnt at school. The practice questions will probably remind you of some of these basics, for example:

The four operators are addition, subtraction, multiplication and division.

The decimal system uses single (units), tens, hundreds, thousands and so on.

Almost every question that you answer will rely on addition, subtraction, multiplication or division. If you always need to write these calculations down on paper you should definitely relearn your multiplication tables – it will save you time and improve your accuracy. As you probably remember from primary school, this involves rote learning. Review the multiplication tables several times a day from a printed copy. If time permits, set yourself the task of memorising at least one table per day.

> review the multiplication tables several times a day

brilliant tip

A good way to test yourself on your multiplication tables is to write them down as quickly as possible. Challenge yourself by trying to do it quicker and quicker. Another good way to practise is reciting the tables to a friend.

Practise involves a high degree of commitment on your part. But when it comes to passing a numeracy test under restricted time conditions, being able to do simple addition, subtraction, multiplication and division in your head will be a huge advantage. It's not a problem if you need to write down long division. (Just be sure to get the decimal columns in the right place!) Remember, though, that each time you do this on a test it is taking up valuable time.

Let's look more closely at how mental arithmetic can help you work more quickly and efficiently. You are not going to need to work out that $12 \times 12 = 144$. But you are going to be faster at working out many simple calculations in your head if, upon seeing numbers such as 14,400, you are confident that:

- this number is divisible by 12 (and hence know that this number must therefore be divisible by both 4 and 3);
- you can apply your multiplication table knowledge to such large numbers;
- you can work out many simple calculations without resorting to a calculator – or even needing to write your calculation down;
- the decimal system and seeing lots of zeros doesn't phase you. You know that 14,400 divided by 12 is merely 144 divided by 12 with an extra couple of zeros added on the end.

The metric system of measurement

The international metric system is based on multiples of 10. For example 10 mm = 1 cm. The metric system covers the weight measures of milligrammes (mg), grammes (g) and kilogrammes (kg); the distance measures of millimetre (mm), centimetre (cm), metre (m) and kilometre (km); and speed (km per hour). If you struggle at times with any of these then you would benefit from asking a friend or relative to explain in full how such measurement systems work.

You need to be able to convert across all measurement terms that are in common usage within the metric system. For example that 1,000 grammes = 1 kilogramme. You also need to know how to convert from one measurement to another. For example, since 60 minutes is the same as 1 hour, then 120 minutes is 2 hours; 101 pence is £1.01, and so on.

There are basic numeracy measurements that you need to be familiar with in order to be able to work with these whenever they are used on a numeracy test question. This is not an exhaustive list, but some of the key measurements – including their abbreviations, which you also need to know – are as follows:

- hours (hrs), minutes (mins) and seconds (s), i.e. 60 seconds in 1 minute and 60 minutes in 1 hour;
- the 24-hour clock, e.g. 13.00 for one o'clock in the afternoon;
- weight measurements i.e. grammes (g) and kilogrammes (kg);
- £ and pence;
- distance (cm, m, miles and km);
- speeds (km per hour and mph);
- volume (1,000 millilitres = 1 litre).

Two of the most common measurements that you are likely to encounter in a numeracy test are the UK monetary system (£ and pence) and time intervals (hours, minutes and seconds), including the 24-hour clock.

⚡ brilliant warning

Don't be caught out by the simple mistake of answering in the wrong units. Read the question carefully to ensure that you are clear about the unit of measurement that the answer requires.

More complex mathemetical operations

Here are some of the more complex mathematical operations that you will need to be able to perform:

- ratios;
- fractions;
- percentages;
- decimals and decimal places;
- exchange rates;
- averages (means) and frequencies (some tests also expect you to work with medians and modes);
- rounding up numbers.

You will need to demonstrate an effective working knowledge of many of these in any numeracy test. Ideally, your performance will improve if you learn to work with them in your head.

Remember that when you have to carry out a string of computations, the multiplication and division calculations take precedence over any addition and subtraction calculations. This is shown in the written form by the use of brackets around the multiplication and division calculations.

The test expects you to be able to work comfortably with large figures. For example, using a comma to separate thousands (i.e. 1,000). Also using the common abbreviations for working with large numbers, e.g. thousands (1,000s or 000s), tens of thousands (10,000s), hundreds of thousands (100,000s) and millions (1,000,000s).

the test expects you to be able to work comfortably with large figures

You may (or may not!) be pleased to see that geometry, prime numbers and calculus are omitted. These forms of maths are unlikely to appear in a numeracy test because they are not commonly used in the workplace.

Expressing numbers in different ways

You need to be comfortable with moving between different ways of expressing numbers – for example changing a number into a percentage or changing a figure shown with decimal places into a fraction. Fractions, decimal points and percentages are just different ways of splitting a number down into smaller divisions. You can think of these as interchangeable. I've given a few examples in the table (in order of increasing size):

Common fractions	Decimal (two decimal places after the decimal point)	Percentage or % (of the number 1)
1/10	0.10	10%
1/5	0.20	20%
1/4	0.25	25%
1/2	0.50	50%
3/4	0.75	75%

If you work best with a particular format, say percentages, then – given the time restrictions on any test – it makes sense for you to use your preference as much as possible. In other words, if you know straight away that 25% is 1/4 of something then it is faster for you to calculate a division by 4 – rather than the standard percentage calculation.

Part II of this book offers many questions to help you to practise expressing numbers in different ways. The detailed answer explanations may tell you to calculate the lowest common denominator. This book, and the test you are preparing to take, assumes that you have a working knowledge of such concepts. However, if you need a reminder of what a common denominator is then you should ask a friend or look this up online. Similarly, if you need to refresh your understanding of decimal points, calculating percentages, the metric system or using the 24-hour clock, there are many helpful websites providing support.

In the individual test chapters I have included website sources of additional information and support.

Working it out

The more complex numerical reasoning questions require the use of a calculator and rough paper for writing down the outcomes of the different calculation stages. Always have plenty of rough paper to use. You might even want to use a fresh

always have plenty of rough paper to use

sheet for each question. When doing the test for real your rough work will not form part of the assessment. It is important to write the question number beside your workings out. That way you are able to return quickly to your calculation if you:

- decide to move on to a different question before reaching the final answer;

- need to use the same early stages of a complex calculation for a subsequent question;

- want to check your answer because it's not shown as one of the answer options;

- need to establish which stage of your calculation is most likely to contain an error.

brilliant warning

Don't get caught out! Remember the effects of compound interest or of a percentage change being made year after year.

Interpreting graphs

Whenever you are presented with a graph or table you will need to interpret this quickly and accurately in order to answer the questions efficiently. It is worth giving the graph or table a quick scan – paying particular attention to the axes – before going on to read the first question.

You need to practise interpreting the following:

● Value of points shown on graphs. This requires reading both the horizontal and vertical axes on a graph. Each of these is commonly divided into segments and will be labelled accordingly. For example, if the graphical axis starts at zero then goes up to 10, then 20, then 30 and so on you know that the divisions on the axis are in blocks of 10.

● Axis titles and keys on graphs. For example a graph that measures *Cost (in £100s)* will provide points on a graph that are a measure of cost in £s. Each figure represents hundreds so a figure three as represented by the graph is being used to represent £300.

If you are worried about pie charts then just think of the different 'pie segments' as fractions of the total value shown.

Seven speedy short cuts

When working with figures and numerical information there are many useful techniques for improving the speed with which you can manipulate figures. For many questions it may well be faster to do the calculations in your head. Here are some handy tips that will help you to save time and reduce your calculator usage.

> it may well be faster to do the calculations in your head

1 Multiplying large figures can be simplified by ignoring the number of zeros and working only with the non-zero figures. So if you need to multiply 22,000 by 5 it is quicker to multiply 22 (the non-zero figures) by 5 = 110. You then add the zeros back on to the answer = 110,000. This technique can also be applied to save time when adding,

subtracting and dividing large figures. To subtract 200 from 5,000 you simply ignore the zeros that are common to both figures. The subtraction then becomes $50 - 2 = 48$. Then add the zeros back on and the answer is 4,800.

2   If you need to multiply by 10, 100 or 1,000 the quickest way to do this is to adjust the number of decimal places. For example, to multiply 67.3 metres by 10, move the decimal point one place to the right ... so 67.3 becomes 673 metres. Similarly, if you are being asked to multiply a figure by 100 or 1,000 you move the decimal points two or three places respectively to the right.

3   When dividing by 10, 100 or 1,000, the quickest way to do this is to adjust the number of decimal places. For instance, if you want to divide $99.9 by 10, move the decimal point one place to the left. So $99.9 becomes $9.99. To divide a figure by 100 or 1,000 just move the decimal point two or three places respectively to the left.

4   When asked to work with numbers that are close to being a 10, 100 or 1,000 then you can round up. You may already do this when you go shopping – for example, you may round up an item costing £3.99 to £4.00. Just remember that you have added 1 pence on to the figure then take account of this fact in your final answer. So if a question concerns the cost of 2 items costing £3.99, you can calculate $2 \times £4.00 = £8.00$ then subtract 2 pence (1 pence for each item) and the total cost $= £8.00 - 2$ pence $= £7.98$.

5   It is sometimes simpler to 'ignore' the decimal places in the figures that you are manipulating. All that you need to do is to check that your answer has the same number of decimal places as figures that you started off with. For example, 1.2 (one decimal place) $\times$ 1.5 (one decimal place) becomes 12 $\times 15 = 180$. Now remember that the answer will need to

have two decimal places, i.e. 1.80. This is a great time-saver, but it is essential to ensure that you put the decimal point back in the right place for the answer.

6   When adding or subtracting large numbers you can just work with the unit numbers (the number furthest to the right, e.g. the 2 on 512) to eliminate some of the multiple choice answer options. For example, 542 + 53 + 444 results in an answer that has the unit number 9 because adding 2 (at the end of 542) to 3 (at the end of 53) and 4 (at the end of 444) equals 9. You can therefore get rid of any answer option that does not end in 9.

7   When you manipulate two or more even numbers (any number ending in 0, 2, 4, 6 or 8) your answer will also be an even number. Whether you add, subtract, divide or multiply two or more even numbers your answer must end in either a number 0, 2, 4, 6 or 8. This is a bit of knowledge that is useful when working under time pressure in a test, because you can ignore any multiple choice answer options that are not even numbers.

How do I practise?

Throughout Part II there are hundreds of practice questions covering each of these areas. The detailed answer explanations will show you how to work with these mathematical operations. See how you get on with the lower-level numeracy practice questions before deciding if you need to relearn any basic mathematical operations. If it becomes clear to you that reading an introduction to arithmetic would be beneficial then I can't recommend strongly enough that you purchase one.

brilliant recap

● You need to get the basics right before moving onto more complex calculations. Start your practice with the first chapter in Part II to reveal how effectively you can cope with basic maths operations.

● Use as many short cuts and time-saving techniques as you can. Being able to do mental arithmetic quickly will be a great help in a timed test situation.

CHAPTER 4

Test-taking tactics

Tick tock ... tick tock ... The countdown begins as soon as you are notified that you will need to take a numeracy test. From that moment onwards, you need to make the most of all the time that you have until the actual test date. You might be planning to do all your preparation in one hit, but I'd strongly advise against this. You will learn and retain more if you undertake several practice sessions instead of just one big session.

It may seem at first that you are only making small gains. But these small gains will soon add up. Think of each practice session as a coin – not worth much on its own, but valuable when you amass several, giving you a wealth of knowledge. Each nugget of information you acquire during your practice sessions will reinforce the others: improving your knowledge in one numerical area will improve your mental agility in other areas.

But preparing for your numeracy test is not just a matter of refreshing your maths skills. How you approach the test itself will also be a major factor in your performance. Fortunately, there are numerous test-taking tactics and techniques that you can learn to give you an edge over the competition. It is especially important for you to familiarise yourself with these if it has been a long time since you have been in a formal test-taking situation.

Familiarise yourself

knowing what to expect on your test day will give you a big advantage

Knowing what to expect on your test day will give you a big advantage, so learn as much as you can about the test you are going to take. Your recruiting organisation may send you practice material in advance of your test. This may be in the form of sample questions, either online or in paper-and-pencil format. The information should also outline why the test is being used in the process and – most importantly – the exact nature of the test that you will be taking on the day. If you are taking the test online you should be provided with contacts for general queries as well as any technical questions relating to the operation of the online system.

This practice opportunity levels the playing field and gives everyone a fair chance – particularly important for people who have not taken a numeracy test before. Make sure you use this material effectively so that you are comfortable with your test format. Ask questions in advance, particularly anything that is unclear on the test instructions. On the test day you will be given the opportunity to go through the administration instructions. But if this knowledge is already stored in your brain, you will feel more comfortable about what you are going to be asked to do on test day.

brilliant tip

If practice material is not sent to you in advance, call your prospective employer and ask for any additional information regarding the test you are going to complete.

Practice strategies

Whether you are learning to play the piano or improving your tennis serve, practice improves your performance. There's a lot of truth to the old adage 'practice makes perfect'. You're not striving for perfection here, but practising questions is known to significantly improve your chances of passing a numeracy test. Allow yourself plenty of time in advance of the real test to complete as many practice test sessions as possible. Continually review what you have learnt from previous practice test sessions so that you use your time most effectively.

Multiple practice sessions

Do not try to do all your preparation in one huge hit. You will learn and retain much more if you undertake several practice sessions instead of one big one. At first it may seem like

> do not try to do all your preparation in one huge hit

you are only making small gains, but these small gains will soon add up to improved numerical reasoning skills.

Take a break

Research has shown that most people's concentration levels drop off after spending longer than forty to fifty minutes in any one practice session. You should plan your practice sessions accordingly. Also, if you start to lose concentration take a short break (of at least a few minutes) and come back to this book later. You'll hopefully come back feeling more focused after making a cup of tea. I know I do!

Learn from your mistakes

Take heed of any simple errors that you keep making throughout your practice session. Make a mental note of these so you can be sure to avoid them in future. It's all too easy to

> it's easy to make sloppy mistakes when you are under pressure

make sloppy mistakes when you are under pressure to perform well and are going through test questions at speed. For example, you should look out for the following:

- Units of measurement, i.e. currency, weight, height. Check that the answer options have the same measurement units as the figures provided in the question and in the table or graph.

- Is the question asking for the answer to be rounded up to one or two decimal places?

- Is the question asking for the answer to be given in £10,000s?

- Is the question stipulating that the answer needs to be a percentage, ratio or fraction?

Stretch yourself

Run through as many practice questions as possible in advance in order to challenge yourself mentally. Don't just focus on those practice questions that you can do quite easily – stretch yourself with harder questions. Undertake timed practice tests on a regular basis to get your brain used to working under pressure.

You might be tempted to review the answers without doing the practice questions yourself. This might seem like a quick win, but be warned! This will save you the time needed to work your way through the book but it *won't* improve your numeracy. The questions on your numeracy test will not be the same as those given here, so you cannot simply learn what the answers will be. You need to digest the underlying strategies and practise the mathematical processes and steps. This takes a time commitment on your part, but is a worthwhile investment if you want to succeed.

 **warning**

Reviewing the answers without attempting the practice questions is a false economy – it will not improve your numeracy skills.

Time-keeping techniques

It is essential to manage your time efficiently in the run-up to the test to ensure you fit in enough practice sessions. But how you use your time *during* the test is also extremely

> how you use your time during the test is extremely important

important. Aim to spend a sufficient amount of time on each question. That's the maximum amount of time that you need to spend in order to get the question correct. No more and no less. More would just be wasting time checking the answer unnecessarily. And less time could lead you to an incorrect answer. If you have time left at the end, go back to check your answers. Start with any questions where you have nagging doubts about the calculation. Do not finish early – go back and double-check your answers if time permits.

OK, so you are not expected to finish the test. You certainly don't need to finish to pass if you get a high number of correct answers. But remember that you will be working under strictly timed exam conditions – like you had to do for school exams. This is a test and calls for an energised approach. If you consider your normal working pace a walk, you should be jogging briskly when you do the test! Pace yourself during the test. To do this you will need to keep an eye on the time remaining. Do a quick check roughly every 10 minutes, checking the time remaining against the number of questions that you have left to answer. Right at the start of the test make a mental note of roughly how long you should be spending on each question. Try to ensure that you do not spend longer than this as you go through each question. Prior to the test you should have considered the number of questions that you would need to answer in the time available. If you have gone through practice questions you will have a good idea of the average time that you need to spend on each question.

You need to motivate yourself to work as efficiently as possible in order to achieve the highest possible score. So . . .

- If you are going too fast then remind yourself not to make any careless mistakes. If you do finish a few minutes before the allotted time is up then you've done very well. Now go back and check those answers you weren't 100% sure about.

- If you are working too slowly then try to speed up. You want to do yourself justice by completing as many questions as you possibly can in the time available.

Don't be a 'hare' by going too fast but equally don't be a 'tortoise' either. Neither will win when it comes to numeracy tests!

brilliant tip

Buy a stopwatch and start timing your practice tests so that you become more aware of your timekeeping and get your brain used to numerical reasoning under pressure. Challenge yourself to do more and more questions in each timed practice session to improve your speed.

Following instructions

misreading the instructions is a very dangerous mistake to make

Misreading the instructions is a very dangerous mistake to make. You must read each word very carefully. If you misinterpret the instructions you could answer several – if not all – questions incorrectly. The administrator is there to answer your questions. If something in the instructions is not what you are expecting or does not make sense to you then check with the administrator before the test timer starts. You don't want to waste time during the test worrying about the instructions when you need to maximise the time you have to complete the questions themselves.

Misreading a question can cost you dearly, too. Even if you've gone through the calculation correctly, it will be wasted time and effort if you've misread any part of the question. A careful reading ensures that your work is being done on a sound footing. I can't stress enough how essential it is to read each word of every question.

brilliant warning

Be sure to fill in your answer sheet *exactly* as instructed. For instance, if it asks you to shade in a circle, don't put a tick or cross in the circle. If your answer sheet is going to be scored by a computer, the machine will only be able to mark a standardised answer sheet.

Top tactics to maximise performance

You are not expected to get a perfect score. Even if you get several answers wrong you can pass the test, as long as a relatively small number of incor-

> you are not expected to get a perfect score

rect answers is outweighed by a much larger number of correct answers. So here are some top test-taking tactics to help you maximise your performance.

- Do not jump ahead. Start by looking at the first question, answer it and then move on to the second. Be methodical. Concentrate your mind on one question at a time.

- You don't want to lose any marks for an incorrect interpretation of the information given. Read each question very carefully and always double-check that you have read across tables, charts and graphs correctly.

- Answer all the questions that you find easy first – as the same credit will be given for each correct answer.

- If you find that you are spending too long on a particular question don't get bogged down. It can be demotivating to spend a long time on one question and then find that you can't reach an answer, or that your answer is not one of the multiple choice options. Remind yourself that there will probably be other questions later in the test that you will find easier to answer. There are a couple of different ways of approaching this:

  - Give your best guess and ensure that you write the question number down next to any workings out so that you can go back to it at the end of the test if time permits.

  - Omit the difficult question completely. The quicker that you decide to do this the better since you will have more time to work on the other questions. That said, it is advisable only to omit those questions that you have no possibility of answering correctly.

- Even when you have a calculator available don't be tempted to double-check your answers or automatically use the calculator on every single question. For time management reasons use your calculator sensibly rather than religiously. On the higher level numerical reasoning tests there will certainly be many questions requiring the use of a calculator. On any given question, only use a calculator if you are likely to make a mistake if you don't use one.

- Follow your intuition if you have a bad feeling about the answer that you have come to. Just because there is a multiple choice option for it does not mean that it is the right answer. If the number just looks too big or too small then check it.

Reviewing your answer options

When doing a multiple-choice numeracy test the answer options are important. If you think about it, they are almost as important as the question that comes before them. Giving them a quick look before starting your calculation at the very least tells you what sort of answer to aim for. Can they help you further to reach the correct answer? Ruling out one or two answer options of a multiple choice question reduces the number of correct answer possibilities. Ask yourself a few questions:

● Are any of the answer options unfeasible? If you have started the numerical calculation in your head, are any of these answer options not of the scale that you expect? If you are going to guess, you have more chance of guessing correctly if you have already ruled out some of the answers as being outside the ballpark. However, if there is time available you should always work out the correct answer rather than guessing blindly – there are deliberately too many answer options for this to be a viable strategy ... otherwise everyone would do it!

● Are any answer options deliberately designed to mislead you? There may be answer options that look very similar to the correct answer – for example, being only a slightly higher or lower value, or where the decimal point is in a different position. Take care not to be caught out by these distractors.

What if my answer just looks wrong?

There are certain things that may indicate that you have made an error somewhere in your calculation. For example, reaching a:

1 *Negative answer.* It is unlikely that the correct answer will be what is called a negative number, i.e. less than zero. In this

book you will only see negative values in some answer explanations to represent a decrease over a period of time. For example, a drop of 5% in sales one month could be expressed as -5%.

2 *Unfeasibly high number*, such as millions of pounds. Questions with charts or tables containing figures of this magnitude usually indicate the scale of the figures with appropriate annotation, such as *in 000,000s*.

3 *Smaller or larger number than the figures given in the question.* Quickly check the scale of the answer you have calculated. If there are single numbers, tens, hundreds or thousands in the data given, then the answer should be in a similar scale.

4 *An answer that just looks wrong.* If this happens you will probably have to start the question again, taking care to recheck the information given, or go back to the last stage of the calculation that you know was correct.

- One helpful shortcut is to just check the single figures at the end of the numbers that you have manipulated to reach your answer. For example, if the question is 35×3 then the answer has to end in a 5 because $(3)5 \times 3 = --5$. This at least allows you to exclude any multiple choice answer options that do not end in 5.

- When doing calculations involving decimal places always ensure that the decimal points are lined up correctly. There's no point using time-saving techniques if you then make a sloppy mistake.

Mental preparation

To maximise your chances of success you need to be able to concentrate 100% on the numeracy test. You need to be in a positive, confident mindset and avoid letting any emotional factors distract or disturb you. Try to maintain perspective. You don't need to get 100% on the numeracy test. You just want to pass and do the best that you can. An optimistic attitude is key. Stay positive: don't get bogged down by

> stay positive: don't get bogged down by negative thinking

negative thinking or obsess about success or failure. You might be afraid that the test will reveal how bad you are at maths. This is a common concern, but worrying about this is a waste of valuable energy. Instead, channel your energy in a positive way – by practising to improve your performance.

Physical preparation

Mental preparation isn't enough – you need to prepare yourself for the test physically, too. Don't worry, you don't need to start doing push-ups or star jumps in addition to all your maths practice – you should just get a good night's sleep before the test. You will concentrate more effectively if you are fully rested. Worried that this might be difficult to achieve? Consider the night before as the final part of a successful test preparation process. If you've done your mental preparation in advance, you don't need to stay up all night cramming; go for a walk, or watch a film, or have a relaxing bath – then turn in early.

Try to take an active approach to the test itself. It may sound like a tall order, but try to enjoy the challenge. On the test day, you need to work as quickly and as accurately as you can. This requires a high level of concentration and motivation. It's important to work hard throughout the whole of the testing period, so pump yourself up in advance. Get psyched! Tell yourself that you are just going to do it!

Dealing with nerves

It is common for people who are unused to taking tests as part of a recruitment process to be quite anxious. Reflect on how you dealt with testing situations in the past. What helped you to stay calm previously? Put all your nervous energy to good use – doing extra practice is probably the best way to steady your nerves. If you believe that you are likely to suffer extreme stress on the day, you could benefit from learning some relaxation techniques.

While feeling a bit nervous is probably inevitable, there are measures you can take to ensure that you are as relaxed as possible on the day:

● Arrive with plenty of time to spare.

● Have everything that you will need with you, including things like reading glasses and hearing aids if you need them.

● Take deep breaths and actually hold your breath for a couple of seconds before exhaling.

⟋ brilliant recap

You can remember the tactics and techniques in this chapter as the acronym **TOP MARK**.

Time Management – it is essential to pace yourself.

Options – can you rule out any answer options?

Practice, practice, practice! Fit in as many practice sessions as you can.

Mental preparation – concentrate 100% on the task in hand.

Attitude – stay positive.

Relax!

Know what to expect on the day.

CHAPTER 5

What else is useful to know in advance?

First, take a moment to consider how far you've come since the first time you picked up this book. Reflecting on the progress you have made should give your confidence a boost. Go on, give yourself a pat on the back! You've learned many useful test-taking strategies; it is nearly time to put them into action. But before that, let's have a look at the test process in general.

Many test publishers and consultancy firms offer British Psychological Society-recognised courses for training test administrators to administer and score numeracy tests in the UK. This maintains the professional standards for conducting group test administration sessions.

Your test administrator should provide you with the following information, in keeping with best practice:

- logistical information, such as directions about how to get to the Test Centre;
- advance notice that you will be taking a numeracy test, including the length of time that the test will take to complete;
- an explanation of the testing process;
- the part that the numeracy test will play in the overall process, including who will have access to your results;
- any feedback arrangements.

If you feel that anything has not been adequately explained to you, or if you are uncomfortable with any aspect of these issues, then don't hesitate to get in touch with the contact name that has been supplied. Remember that your prospective employer or place of study will want to ensure that you are treated fairly throughout the testing process. That means from the time when you are notified that you need to undertake a numeracy test right up to the time that you find out the outcome.

don't make any assumptions – if anything is unclear check before proceeding

Don't make any assumptions – if anything is unclear check before proceeding. The administrator is there to answer your questions.

What does the test administrator do on the day?

In order for the test results to be reliable and fair, the test session needs to be standardised. That means the onus is on the test administrator to make sure you do what you are supposed to do and follow all the instructions exactly. Ask the administrator about anything that is not clear, particularly the practice questions. Make sure that everything is clear *before* the timer starts since you will not be allowed to ask any questions once the test has started.

Everyone taking the test must do the following:

- Complete the practice questions at the start of the test (in the initial 10–20 minutes). The administrator will ensure that every applicant present at the session completes the practice questions. The administrator will go through any of the practice questions if you are unclear as to how an answer was arrived at.

- Start the test at exactly the same time. You need to follow the administrator's instructions to the letter. Do not start until you are told to do so.

● Stop working as soon as the test administrator says that the test has finished.

 **warning**

Just as you would not be late for an interview, you should not be late for a test. Don't assume that you can be fitted in at whatever time you arrive. Your testing time will have been scheduled in so there's probably someone using your computer before and after you.

How are my test results used?

Your prospective employer or place of study expects that there will be range of test scores on the numeracy test. That's why the test is being used in the first place – to differentiate between applicants in terms of their numerical reasoning ability.

A couple of comparisons are made:

1 Each individual's overall score is compared to a large group of hundreds – sometimes thousands – of similar applicants who have taken the same test before. This is the norm group – the normal range of scores that are typical of the type of people who sit the test. This way, your individual score is given in a meaningful way for that particular test.

2 At the same time, there is a particular group of applicants who took the test around the same time as you did. The pass mark is also likely to be based on how these other applicants performed. It may go up or down depending on the number of vacancies for a particular job or course or on the number of applicants who have applied.

> your numeracy test may be one stage in a long recruitment process

Your numeracy test may be one stage in a long recruitment process. It will be used to screen out unsuitable applicants who do not have the necessary level of numerical reasoning ability. This process is called a sifting out or de-selection process.

How does online testing work?

The use of online testing has increased dramatically over the last few years. The most obvious difference between this and a paper-and-pencil test is that you take the test on a computer. From the administrator's perspective, this presents some complications.

One of the main concerns with online testing is proving that the person who takes the test is the same person who has applied. For proof of identification reasons you may need to complete an online test at a special testing centre. If you complete the test in the comfort of your own home, you will certainly be asked to use a log-in and password (delivered to you separately) and the chances are that you will also be asked to undertake a further test session at a subsequent date – to show that you do indeed have the numerical reasoning ability needed to pass the test.

> you may need to complete an online test at a special testing centre

The British Psychological Society and the International Test Commission guidelines on computer-based and internet-delivered testing list the following four types of testing environment:

1   *Open mode* – where there is no means of identifying who is taking the test. This could be a practice test website where you do not need to enter a user ID and password before proceeding.

2   *Controlled mode* – where the test is only available to known

users who must request and receive a user ID and password before they can proceed any further.

3   *Supervised mode* – where a test administrator supervises the test session and authenticates the identity of every test-taker present.

4   *Managed mode* – this features an even higher level of human supervision, typically at a dedicated Test Centre that strictly controls the test-taking environment.

 **warning**

Do not be tempted to cheat by getting someone else to do the test as you will be retested further on in the process!

Adaptive tests

Some online numeracy tests are adaptive tests. These are complex, and potentially difficult, tests that can be used to differentiate between high-level graduate job roles. The simplest types of adaptive numeracy tests are just different variants of the test at different difficulty levels. In more complex adaptive testing set-ups, the questions deliberately adapt to how you are performing as you progress through the test. So if you are doing well, you will find that the questions get progressively harder. This allows your numerical reasoning ability to be thoroughly tested until you reach the maximum level at which you can answer questions correctly and within the time constraints.

Tips for taking online tests

● Online tests that you complete at home allow you as much time as you like to read the instructions onscreen. Make sure that you are absolutely clear on what you are being asked to do as there is no administrator to answer your questions. Take as much time as you need – you won't be keeping anyone waiting.

- You'll be the only person in the room, but that doesn't mean that you control the time allowed on the test. Once you have started you need to complete the test in the allotted time. You can take a break whenever you need to but it will cost you valuable time.

- A well-designed online test will have been thoroughly tested to work on most computers. You should be told the PC specification and internet access requirements in advance. But if you do have an access problem at any stage, use the contact information provided onscreen or contact the person who sent you the invitation.

- If you do not have internet access at home, be resourceful: think about alternative venues for taking the test. For example, you could complete the test on a relative's computer or at a local library. Your local internet café might be another option, though it will most likely be quite noisy.

- Just in case your computer is not behaving on the day, it makes sense not to leave taking the test to the last minute.

Will I get any feedback?

Feedback may take several forms and should always be provided to you. It is important to remember that it is your relative performance that has been measured – meaning how your performance compared with the large norm group that have taken the test before. You won't receive marks out of 10 or a percentage score as you might expect. Instead, your feedback could be one of the following:

- A standardised score such as a percentile. This is similar to a percentage but the 60th percentile means that you did better than 60% of the norm group.

● A band that compares you to the norm group – for example, average or above average. Remember, the term 'average' refers to average within a group of people similar to you who have taken the test for similar reasons to yourself. Your results are not being compared to the general population. So, a 'slightly below average' or 'below average' grade doesn't mean that you are worse than everyone else in the general population.

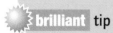 **tip**

It is best practice in the testing industry to provide feedback. Request this if you are not offered it.

How will fairness be ensured?

If you have a disability, then be sure to inform your prospective employer or educational establishment in advance if you require any adaptations to the testing process. It is likely that you will have been asked this question on your application

> if you have a disability, inform your prospective employer or educational establishment in advance

form. You may also have been asked to complete a separate Equal Opportunities or monitoring form. Let them know how you have approached testing in the past and what provisions need to be made to ensure that you have equal access to the numeracy test. This includes the format of the test, the medium through which it is communicated, and how it is communicated. Adaptations can be made to the numeracy testing process whenever it is appropriate to do so, including an additional time allowance and having the questions delivered in Braille or large print.

How do I behave on the day?

Relax . . . Staying calm and positive is the best way to approach your test. If you've read this book you will have done plenty of practice questions and have many strategies to use.

 recap

- The test administrator is there to ensure that the process is standardised for fairness. He or she is also there to answer your questions before the timed test begins.

- When taking an online test – either at home or at a Test Centre – there are certain considerations you should be aware of.

- Feedback should always be provided and can take different forms – and compares your performance to that of a norm group.

Summary

After reading through this first part of the book, you should be feeling confident that you know what a numeracy test entails and how best to prepare for taking one. The chapters in Part 1 have given you an artillery of maths short cuts and test-taking techniques to deploy on the big day. Now it is up to you to tackle the practice questions in the Part 2. Just in case you are feeling daunted by the task in hand, or unsure about whether to put in the effort, let me quickly remind you about the benefits associated with practice.

1   Practising with the correct test format is known to improve performance. Part 2 offers you the opportunity to do this, and also to extend your practice to other similar numeracy test formats.

2   Practice will increase your confidence. This will help your focus and concentration levels during the test.

3   Practice will help you to develop your test-taking strategies.

4   Practice leads to a more efficient approach. Your aim is to make the most effective use of the available time – working at speed, but not at the expense of accuracy. It's a big ask and it requires lots of practice.

Those are pretty convincing reasons, right? So what are you waiting for? Turn over to Part 2 and start putting your newly refreshed numeracy skills into action. You owe it to yourself to do the very best you can.

Time to practise

This part of the book is all about practising. Here's where you will find examples of the most popular numeracy test formats used in Britain. Keep reminding yourself that it's essential to practise as much as possible. It is worth putting in the effort when entry to a future profession is at stake. In addition to the practice test questions, there are lots of helpful hints, tips and strategies scattered throughout this section. Be sure to read them, as they suggest great ways to improve your overall performance.

If you know your test format then you can go straight to the relevant chapter. For example, if you are preparing to take the UKCAT and only want to practise for this test, head straight for the UKCAT practice questions.

The following role-specific numeracy tests are featured in this section:

- the Armed Forces:
  - Army BARB (Chapter 6);
  - Royal Navy RT (Chapter 6);
  - RAF AST (Chapter 6);
- Qualified Teacher Status (QTS) Numeracy Skills Test (Chapter 7);
- The UK Clinical Aptitude Test for Medical and Dental Degrees (UKCAT) (Chapter 8).

Other readers may only know that they will be taking a general graduate-level or a senior managerial-level numeracy test. In this case, you should start with the chapter containing practice tests at that level of difficulty. Chapter 9 features practice test questions at the graduate level while the questions in Chapter 10 are aimed at the senior managerial level.

If you don't know your test format, choose a format that most closely resembles the difficulty level. If you are a beginner, I suggest you start with Chapter 6 and work through as many of the subsequent chapters as you can. Be selective if you like and dip into other practice chapters. Maybe you want more practice at percentages. You can cherry pick questions dealing with percentages from several different chapters. The start of each chapter includes a handy summary of what each test assesses.

The questions appear in a rough order of increasing difficulty. If the practice questions you started with are too difficult you can always go back to complete the earlier chapters. Equally, feel free to skip ahead if you find the questions too easy. Stretch yourself by trying the practice tests in subsequent chapters – these harder questions will help sharpen your numerical abilities.

For each test format there are many realistic practice questions, mirroring the different types of questions that are likely to come up on the actual test. At the end of each chapter, there are answers for every question, along with detailed step-by-step calculations where needed.

CHAPTER 6

The Armed Forces

I t takes more than a willingness to serve your country to enlist in the British armed forces. In addition to demonstrating your physical fitness and proof of British residency, you must also take aptitude tests in order to be eligible to join the Army, the Royal Navy and the Royal Air Force. Numeracy plays a key part in the jobs of many service personnel, for example engineers, technicians and logistical experts. And for a soldier in a combat situation, the ability to work with numbers efficiently could be a matter of life or death. Thus each of the Armed Forces includes a numeracy test component. Each set of questions in the following section will be useful practice for candidates hoping to enter any of the armed forces.

The Army: The British Army Recruitment Battery (BARB)

So you want 'to be the best'? All recruits to the British Army start by taking a computerised battery of five tests – the British Army Recruitment Battery (BARB). The BARB is a touch-screen test. It assesses your ability to analyse information accurately and logically. The BARB is not timed – the computer will adjust the number of questions as you go along, based on how quickly you are answering them. It usually takes about thirty minutes to do the entire battery.

How is it used?

The results of the BARB provide the Army with useful information on an applicant's training requirements. A candidate's score on the BARB test, based on the number of correct answers and the time taken to complete it, is called their GTI (General Trainability Index). The BARB does not operate on a pass/fail basis. Rather, it identifies suitable career options. A higher score on the BARB ensures a greater choice of career options.

What does it test?

The five tests comprising the BARB are:

1   Reasoning;

2   Letter Checking;

3   Number Distance;

4   Odd One Out;

5   Symbol Rotation.

Below you will find practice questions for the Number Distance portion of the BARB.

⌕ brilliant resources

Seach the Government's Directgov website for useful information on the role, the qualifications required and how to apply:

http://careersadvice.direct.gov.uk/helpwithyourcareer/jobprofiles/

You can also visit the Army's website for more information:

http://www.army.mod.uk/join

Instructions

Review the set of three numbers given in each question. Which is the largest number? Which is the smallest number? This leaves one other number remaining. Your answer is the number that is furthest away from this remaining number.

I recommend that you immediately identify the lowest and the highest numbers as soon as you see the row of three numbers appear. Then focus your attention on the third number – the one that is neither the highest nor the lowest. Next, establish which of these two numbers is furthest away from the third number in the question by comparing the two subtraction calculations. Finally, select the answer option that is the number that is furthest away.

 **example**

Question 1.

The computer screen will show you three numbers for each question, as follows:

1   8   5

The answer options that will then appear on screen are as follows.

(A) 1   (B) 8   (C) 5

You need to work out the middle number by a process of excluding the largest and smallest numbers. This is 5.

You need to find which of the other two numbers in the question (1 and 8) is furthest away from this middle number (5). The answer is 1.

The answers on page 109 may help you in this since they show you the sequence of steps to use. Just follow the columns across, with each new column representing the next step.

brilliant tip

You need to work through as many of the questions as you can as quickly and as accurately as possible. Don't make the mistake of going too slowly. Make a firm decision without the need to go back and double-check it.

Practice questions

2. 5   9   3
   (A) 5   (B) 9   (C) 3

3. 7   5   1
   (A) 7   (B) 5   (C) 1

4. 7   12   6
   (A) 7   (B) 12   (C) 6

5. 9   6   1
   (A) 9   (B) 6   (C) 1

6. 3   14   8
   (A) 3   (B) 14   (C) 8

7. 16   12   9
   (A) 16   (B) 12   (C) 9

8. 1   18   8
   (A) 1   (B) 18   (C) 8

9. 19   13   8
   (A) 19   (B) 13   (C) 8

10. 7   12   9
    (A) 7   (B) 12   (C) 9

11. 3   6   8
    (A) 3   (B) 6   (C) 8

12. 12   5   3
    (A) 12   (B) 5   (C) 3

13. 9   5   11
    (A) 9   (B) 5   (C) 11

14. 7   5   1
    (A) 7   (B) 5   (C) 1

15. 15   2   7
    (A) 15   (B) 2   (C) 7

16. 2   17   10
    (A) 2   (B) 17   (C) 10

17. 3   16   11
    (A) 3   (B) 16   (C) 11

18. 9   17   8
    (A) 9   (B) 17   (C) 8

19. 12   19   9
    (A) 12   (B) 19   (C) 9

20. 8   3   18
    (A) 8   (B) 3   (C) 18

21. 12   6   1
    (A) 12   (B) 6   (C) 1

22. 5   11   7
    (A) 5   (B) 11   (C) 7

23. 2   9   14
    (A) 2   (B) 9   (C) 14

24. 3   16   8
    (A) 3   (B) 16   (C) 8

25. 2   20   12
    (A) 2   (B) 20   (C) 12

The answers to these questions are on page 109

The Royal Navy: The Standard Naval Entrance Test

The Standard Naval Entrance Test, or Recruiting Test (RT), is a battery of four multiple-choice tests covering the following areas:

1   reasoning;

2   verbal ability;

3   numeracy;

4   mechanical comprehension.

The test is completed in a paper-and-pencil format. Each sub-test is timed separately by a trained test administrator and the whole thing takes about an hour to complete. Two of the sub-tests have a numerical element: the numeracy test and the reasoning test. In the real test a trained test administrator will read through the instructions for each sub-test before you start.

How is it used?

The Royal Navy's recruitment is a staged process. You must successfully complete one stage before you move on to the next. A successful performance on the RT means you will go on to have a selection interview. The pass mark for the test varies depending on which branch you are applying to join – for example, the most technical branches will require a higher pass mark. But for many of the branches, a mark of 50% is acceptable.

⤢ brilliant resources

There is a sample practice test booklet available on the official Royal Navy website:

http://www.royalnavy.mod.uk/server/show/nav.6259

This is a very useful source of additional practice. I highly recommended that you download it, read through the information and complete the additional practice questions.

Search the Government's Directgov website for useful information on the role, the qualifications required and how to apply:

http://careersadvice.direct.gov.uk/helpwithyourcareer/jobprofiles/

Navy RT – Reasoning
What does it test?

The reasoning test has 30 questions and lasts 9 minutes. It tests your ability to process information, identify relationships and differentiate between relevant and irrelevant information. The reasoning test features several different types of questions: verbal reasoning, spatial reasoning and abstract reasoning, as well as numerical reasoning. The number series practice questions that follow deal *only* with the numerical reasoning portion of this sub-test.

Instructions

Consider the sequence of numbers and work out which number comes next. The first thing that you need to do is to work out the relationship between the first and second, second and third numbers and so on. The main sequences are going to be based on addition, subtraction, multiplication or sometimes division.

If you can't get the pattern straight away then I recommend using a systematic step-by-step approach.

1   Start by calculating the difference between the first and second, and the second and third numbers. Can you see a pattern? If so, it is likely to be a pattern based upon addition or subtraction. For example:

- Is the sequence based upon adding the same number each time (e.g. adding 2 to the number each time)?

- Is the sequence based upon adding two numbers together each time (e.g. adding the previous two numbers together each time)?

- Is the sequence based upon subtracting the same number each time (e.g. subtracting 2 from the number each time)?

2   If the series does not appear to be based upon addition or subtraction then the next option to consider is that it is based upon multiplication – for example, multiplying by the same number each time.

3   If this doesn't provide a solution then consider whether it looks like two different series of numbers – rather than the more commonly found single series.

4   Now you need to start thinking outside of the box. Try not to think in terms of the traditional counting system 1, 2, 3 . . .

brilliant tip

You need to be able to complete at least three questions on average in a minute. Time yourself and see how close you are to achieving this benchmark.

Practice questions

1   Consider this sequence of numbers
11, 9, 7, 5, 3 . . .
Which number comes next?
(A) 1
(B) 2

(C) 3

(D) 4

(E) 5

2   Consider this sequence of numbers
5, 20, 35, 50, 65, 80 . . .
Which number comes next?

(A) 70

(B) 75

(C) 85

(D) 90

(E) 95

3   Consider this sequence of numbers
4, 8, 16, 32, 64 . . .
Which number comes next?

(A) 80

(B) 96

(C) 128

(D) 144

(E) 170

4   Consider this sequence of numbers
3, 6, 9, 12, 15 . . .
Which number comes next?

(A) 16

(B) 17

(C) 18

(D) 19

(E) 20

5   Consider this sequence of numbers
5, 10, 15, 20, 25 . . .
Which number comes next?

(A) 26

(B) 27

(C) 28

(D) 29

(E) 30

6   Consider this sequence of numbers
90, 77, 64, 51, 38 ...
Which number comes next?

(A) 25

(B) 27

(C) 29

(D) 31

(E) 33

7   Consider this sequence of numbers
21, 36, 51, 66, 81 ...
Which number comes next?

(A) 89

(B) 92

(C) 94

(D) 96

(E) 99

8   Consider this sequence of numbers
83, 71, 59, 47, 35 ...
Which number comes next?

(A) 29

(B) 25

(C) 23

(D) 21

(E) 17

9   Consider this sequence of numbers
5, 10, 17, 26, 37 ...
Which number comes next?

(A) 39

(B) 42

(C) 45

(D) 47

(E) 50

10 Consider this sequence of numbers
    2, 7, 4, 8, 6, 9 ...
    Which number comes next?
    (A) 7
    (B) 8
    (C) 9
    (D) 10
    (E) 11

11 Consider this sequence of numbers
    36, 48, 60, 72, 84 ...
    Which number comes next?
    (A) 96
    (B) 97
    (C) 98
    (D) 99
    (E) 100

12 Consider this sequence of numbers
    5, 3, 20, 6, 35, 9, 50 ...
    Which number comes next?
    (A) 65
    (B) 45
    (C) 25
    (D) 15
    (E) 12

13 Consider this sequence of numbers
    25, 23, 20, 16, 11 ...
    Which number comes next?
    (A) 9
    (B) 8
    (C) 7
    (D) 6
    (E) 5

14   Consider this sequence of numbers
     24, 33, 42, 51, 60 . . .
     Which number comes next?
     (A) 66
     (B) 67
     (C) 68
     (D) 69
     (E) 70

15   Consider this sequence of numbers
     3, 5, 6, 10, 9, 20 . . .
     Which number comes next?
     (A) 11
     (B) 12
     (C) 15
     (D) 25
     (E) 30

16   Consider this sequence of numbers
     1, 2, 6, 24, 120 . . .
     Which number comes next?
     (A) 720
     (B) 360
     (C) 240
     (D) 144
     (E) 126

17   Consider this sequence of numbers
     1, 2, 5, 14, 41 . . .
     Which number comes next?
     (A) 51
     (B) 72
     (C) 81
     (D) 92
     (E) 122

18 Consider this sequence of numbers
    12, 3, 15, 7, 18, 11 ...
    Which number comes next?
    (A) 23
    (B) 21
    (C) 19
    (D) 17
    (E) 14

19 Consider this sequence of numbers
    201, 30, 191, 40, 181, 50 ...
    Which number comes next?
    (A) 60
    (B) 70
    (C) 171
    (D) 180
    (E) 181

20 Consider this sequence of numbers
    1, 5, 25, 125 ...
    Which number comes next?
    (A) 130
    (B) 150
    (C) 250
    (D) 375
    (E) 625

21 Consider this sequence of numbers
    2, 20, 38, 56 ...
    Which number comes next?
    (A) 65
    (B) 74
    (C) 76
    (D) 83
    (E) 92

22   Consider this sequence of numbers
     2, 7, 13, 20, 28 . . .
     Which number comes next?
     (A) 34
     (B) 35
     (C) 36
     (D) 37
     (E) 38

23   Consider this sequence of numbers
     4, 10, 5, 9, 6, 8 . . .
     Which number comes next?
     (A) 11
     (B) 10
     (C) 9
     (D) 8
     (E) 7

24   Consider this sequence of numbers
     2, 4, 10, 28, 82 . . .
     Which number comes next?
     (A) 244
     (B) 164
     (C) 110
     (D) 92
     (E) 84

25   Consider this sequence of numbers
     9, 25, 7, 30, 5, 35 . . .
     Which number comes next?
     (A) 40
     (B) 33
     (C) 23
     (D) 13
     (E) 3

The answers to these questions are on pages 110–14

Navy RT – Numeracy
What does it test?

The numeracy portion of the RT consists of 30 questions that you must complete in 16 minutes. It does not require the use of a calculator. This is a test of how quickly and accurately you can complete basic mathematical operations, such as addition, subtraction, multiplication and division. The test also requires you to show that you can quickly and accurately use fractions, percentages and basic algebra.

Instructions

Choose the correct answer from the multiple choice options shown. In the real test you will have a separate answer sheet on which to complete your answers. You indicate the correct answer by crossing through that letter. Make sure that you only mark one answer per question. If you decide to change your answer, blacken out your original answer then cross through the letter for your new answer. Focus on working accurately whilst also trying to complete as many questions as you can.

brilliant tips

- You need to be able to complete roughly two questions on average in a minute. Time yourself and see how close you are to achieving this benchmark.

- It is better to guess than to leave a question unanswered as you do not lose marks for an incorrect answer. The same applies to the other sub-tests of the RT.

Practice questions

1   What is the number 55.368 to two decimal places?
   (A) 55.30
   (B) 55.35
   (C) 55.36
   (D) 55.37
   (E) 55.40

2   Add 456 to 9322
   (A) 9678
   (B) 9687
   (C) 9778
   (D) 9787
   (E) 9788

3   What is 40% of 5000?
   (A) 2000
   (B) 2500
   (C) 3000
   (D) 3500
   (E) 4000

4   A garden measures 20 metres by 15 metres. What is the area
   of the garden, in square metres?
   (A) 150 square metres
   (B) 200 square metres
   (C) 250 square metres
   (D) 300 square metres
   (E) 350 square metres

5   Subtract 99.1 from 144.9
   (A) 45.9
   (B) 45.8
   (C) 45.7
   (D) 45.6
   (E) 45.5

6   What is 0.40 expressed as a percentage of 1?
    (A) 4%
    (B) 14%
    (C) 24%
    (D) 34%
    (E) 40%

7   17.5% of the cost of buying a new printer is VAT. If a new printer costs £50.00 without VAT, then how much is the VAT?
    (A) £8.75
    (B) £17.50
    (C) £50.00
    (D) £58.75
    (E) £67.50

8   77 × 3 = ?
    (A) 211
    (B) 221
    (C) 231
    (D) 241
    (E) 251

9   A ninth of a family's monthly budget is spent on gas and electricity bills. If the average cost per month of gas and electricity bills is £90 then how much is the monthly budget?
    (A) £800
    (B) £810
    (C) £890
    (D) £900
    (E) £990

10   What is 40% of 500?
    (A) 100
    (B) 150
    (C) 200
    (D) 250
    (E) 300

11   0.25 × 2.6 = ?
      (A) 0.69
      (B) 0.68
      (C) 0.67
      (D) 0.66
      (E) 0.65

12   A salesman leaves his house at 9.00 and travels 100 miles to get to his client meeting at 11.00 hrs. What is his average speed?
      (A) 35 mph
      (B) 40 mph
      (C) 45 mph
      (D) 50 mph
      (E) 55 mph

13   What is the number 15.6844 to three decimal places?
      (A) 15.680
      (B) 15.684
      (C) 15.685
      (D) 15.690
      (E) 15.700

14   What is 0.40 expressed as a fraction?
      (A) ⅘
      (B) ⅗
      (C) ⅖
      (D) ⅕
      (E) ⅒

15   200 × 0.25 = ?
      (A) 50
      (B) 55
      (C) 60
      (D) 65
      (E) 70

16 $\frac{1}{3} \times \frac{1}{8} = ?$
(A) $\frac{2}{3}$
(B) $\frac{1}{3}$
(C) $\frac{2}{8}$
(D) $\frac{1}{8}$
(E) $\frac{1}{24}$

17 What is 70% expressed as a decimal?
(A) 0.9
(B) 0.8
(C) 0.7
(D) 0.6
(E) 0.5

18 What is 0.10 expressed as a fraction?
(A) $\frac{1}{4}$
(B) $\frac{1}{5}$
(C) $\frac{1}{8}$
(D) $\frac{1}{10}$
(E) $\frac{1}{100}$

19 $410 \times 80 = ?$
(A) 3,280
(B) 3,820
(C) 32,800
(D) 38,200
(E) 38,800

20 A woman works a seven-hour day five days of the week and then works three hours' overtime over the weekend. What is the total number of hours that she works that week?
(A) 38
(B) 39
(C) 40
(D) 41
(E) 42

The answers to these questions are on pages 114–16

The Royal Air Force: The Airman Selection Test (AST)

Applying to the RAF is a process that takes several months from initial application through to acceptance. The staged selection process involves interviews, a fitness test, and of course, aptitude tests. The tests that you are asked to take will depend upon the particular RAF career that you are applying for: officer, non-commissioned aircrew or airman/airwoman. This practice test aims to prepare you for the numerical reasoning components of the Airman Selection Test.

The RAF's Airman Selection Test (AST) is used as part of the process for becoming an airman/airwoman. The AST comprises the following seven multiple choice tests:

1 Verbal Reasoning

2 Numerical Reasoning

3 Work Rate

4 Spatial Reasoning

5 Electrical Comprehension

6 Mechanical Comprehension

7 Memory

Brilliant Resources

As well as general test details there is a sample airman/airwoman selection text, containing examples of each type of aptitude question at: www.raf.mod.uk/careers/aptitude/aptitude.html

How is it used?

If you pass the AST you will progress to the next recruitment stage – the health assessment.

What does it test?

The Numerical Reasoning portion of the AST is in two parts. The first part (which I am calling RAF 1) assesses your ability to use fractions and decimals. You are given 4 minutes to answer 12 questions. The second part (RAF 2) assesses your ability to interpret graphs and tables. There are 15 questions to answer in 11 minutes.

RAF 1

brilliant tips

- Try the other Armed Forces numeracy questions to get additional practice.
- You need to be able to complete three questions on average in a minute. Time yourself and see how close you are to achieving this benchmark.

Instructions

Choose the correct answer from the multiple choice options shown.

Practice questions

1   $50 \times 0.5 = ?$
   (A) 15
   (B) 20
   (C) 25
   (D) 30
   (E) 35

2   $0.98 + 0.47 = ?$
   (A) 1.48
   (B) 1.47
   (C) 1.46

    (D) 1.45

    (E) 1.44

3   432 + 88 = ?

    (A) 520

    (B) 516

    (C) 513

    (D) 510

    (E) 500

4    $12 \times 200 = ?$

    (A) 2,300

    (B) 2,400

    (C) 2,500

    (D) 2,600

    (E) 2,700

5   0.66 − 0.23 = ?

    (A) 0.53

    (B) 0.51

    (C) 0.48

    (D) 0.43

    (E) 0.33

6    $\frac{1}{3} \times 33 = ?$

    (A) 11

    (B) 13

    (C) 15

    (D) 18

    (E) 23

7   225 − 44 = ?

    (A) 197

    (B) 191

    (C) 187

    (D) 181

    (E) 177

8    $0.5 \times 36 = ?$
   (A) 14
   (B) 16
   (C) 18
   (D) 20
   (E) 22

9    $15 \times \frac{1}{3} = ?$
   (A) 4
   (B) 5
   (C) 6
   (D) 7
   (E) 8

10   $0.45 \times 200 = ?$
   (A) 70
   (B) 75
   (C) 80
   (D) 85
   (E) 90

11   What is 31.456 expressed to two decimal places?
   (A) 31.40
   (B) 31.45
   (C) 31.46
   (D) 31.50
   (E) 31.60

12   $\frac{1}{3} + \frac{1}{2} = ?$
   (A) $\frac{7}{9}$
   (B) $\frac{7}{8}$
   (C) $\frac{5}{6}$
   (D) $\frac{4}{6}$
   (E) $\frac{2}{3}$

13   $46 / 4.6 = ?$
   (A) 4
   (B) 6

    (C) 8

    (D) 10

    (E) 12

14 $\frac{1}{4} \times 600 = ?$

    (A) 125

    (B) 150

    (C) 175

    (D) 200

    (E) 225

15 $0.25 \times 0.5 = ?$

    (A) 0.120

    (B) 0.125

    (C) 0.130

    (D) 0.135

    (E) 0.140

16 $90 + 0.99 = ?$

    (A) 90.09

    (B) 90.90

    (C) 90.99

    (D) 99.09

    (E) 99.99

17 $550 / 11 = ?$

    (A) 50

    (B) 49

    (C) 48

    (D) 47

    (E) 46

18 $5.5 \times 9.5 = ?$

    (A) 51.25

    (B) 51.75

    (C) 52.25

    (D) 52.50

    (E) 52.75

19   ¼ × 500 = ?
  (A) 125
  (B) 150
  (C) 175
  (D) 200
  (E) 225

20   What is 30% of 250?
  (A) 60
  (B) 65
  (C) 70
  (D) 75
  (E) 80

The answers to these questions are on page 116–17

RAF 2

Instructions

You will be presented with numerical information in the form of a chart or table, followed by a series of five questions. Use the data from the table or chart to choose the correct answer from the multiple choice options shown. You need to be able to complete three questions on average every two minutes. Time yourself and see how close you are to achieving this benchmark.

brilliant tip

For additional practice with questions involving graphs, statistical tables and charts, you can try doing the graduate and senior managerial practice tests in Chapters 9 and 10 as these also require interpretation of complex numerical data.

Practice questions

Refer to the table's prices of a set of items at a local newsagents compared to a supermarket to answer questions 1–5.

Prices of a set of items at local newsagents compared to a supermarket

Item	Price (local newsagents)	Price (supermarket)
TV guide magazine	80p	80p
Bag of crisps	40p	30p
Tin of soup	66p	59p
Celebrity magazine	£1.25	£1.25
Greetings card	£1.99	£1.49
Loaf of bread	£1.15	99p

1   A shopper buys two greetings cards, four tins of soup and a loaf of bread from the local newsagents. What is the total cost of their purchases?

   (A) £5.96
   (B) £6.33
   (C) £7.11
   (D) £7.77
   (E) £8.11

2   How much change from £5.00 does a shopper get who buys three bags of crisps and a TV Guide from the supermarket?

   (A) £3.10
   (B) £3.15
   (C) £3.20
   (D) £3.25
   (E) £3.30

3   What is the difference in price between a bag of crisps and a greetings card at the newsagents compared to the supermarket?

   (A) 60p more

(B) 50p more

(C) 70p less

(D) 50p less

(E) 60p less

4   How many items cost the same at both the supermarket and the newsagents?

(A) 1

(B) 2

(C) 3

(D) 4

(E) 5

5   Which items cost over 20% more at the newsagents compared to the supermarket?

(A) Loaf of bread and greetings card

(B) Bag of crisps and greetings card

(C) Tin of soup and TV guide magazine

(D) Celebrity magazine and tin of soup

(E) Loaf of bread and bag of crisps

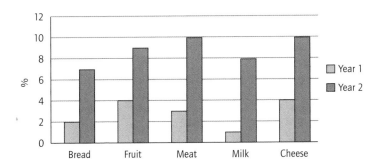

Refer to the graph showing the % increases in the average price of five types of food produce (Years 1 and 2) to answer questions 6–10.

6   Which food product increased by the smallest % in Year 1?

(A) Bread

(B) Fruit

(C) Meat

(D) Milk

(E) Cheese

7   The average cost of bread at the start of Year 1 is £1.10. What is the average cost of bread at the end of Year 1 (to the nearest pence)?

(A) £1.10

(B) £1.11

(C) £1.12

(D) £1.13

(E) £1.14

8   Which food products increased by more than 8% in Year 2?

(A) Bread, fruit and cheese

(B) Fruit, meat and cheese

(C) Fruit, meat, milk and cheese

(D) Meat, milk and cheese

(E) Meat and cheese

9   Which two food products increased by 4% in Year 1?

(A) Bread and cheese

(B) Meat and cheese

(C) Fruit and meat

(D) Meat and milk

(E) Fruit and cheese

10   The average cost of cheese at the end of Year 2 is £2.75. What was the average cost at the end of Year 1?

(A) £2.50

(B) £2.55

(C) £2.60

(D) £2.65

(E) £2.70

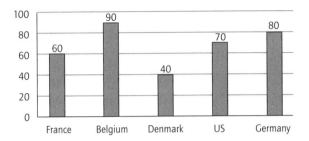

To answer questions 11–15 refer to the graph showing the *Confectionery imports to the UK (£ millions)* from various countries.

11 Which countries have the highest and the lowest confectionery exports to the UK?
(A) France and Belgium
(B) Belgium and Denmark
(C) Germany and Denmark
(D) Belgium and France
(E) Germany and Belgium

12 From which countries is the level of confectionery imports more than 20% of the French level?
(A) US and Belgium
(B) Belgium, US and Germany
(C) Belgium
(D) US and Germany
(E) Belgium and Germany

13 The level of confectionery imports from Denmark increases by a ¼. What is the new amount (£ millions)?
(A) 42
(B) 45
(C) 48
(D) 50
(E) 60

14   What is the total amount of confectionery imports across
       the five countries (£ millions)?
       (A) 300
       (B) 320
       (C) 340
       (D) 360
       (E) 380

15   The amount of confectionery imports from the US doubled
       in the next year. What is the new level of confectionery
       imports from the US (£ millions)?
       (A) 120
       (B) 125
       (C) 130
       (D) 135
       (E) 140

Use the table of the cost of holiday mini-breaks to seaside hotels
to answer questions 16–20.

Cost of holiday mini-breaks to seaside hotels

	2 nights	4 nights
St Ives – Kings Hotel	£140	£229
Eastbourne – Prior Hotel	£95	£175
Newquay – Major Hotel	£120	£215
Brighton – Bains Hotel	£110	£189
Bexhill – Eddy's Hotel	£99	£165
Brighton – Dune Roaming Hotel	£115	£205

16   A surfer is planning a holiday that takes in two nights at the
       Major Hotel in Newquay and four nights at the Kings Hotel
       in St Ives. What would the total cost be?
       (A) £290
       (B) £315
       (C) £349
       (D) £355
       (E) £369

17 A couple is planning to spend four nights at Eastbourne (Prior Hotel). What is the total cost of their stay?
    (A) £165
    (B) £175
    (C) £215
    (D) £229
    (E) £350

18 A father plans to stay with his son – who pays ½ price – for two nights at Newquay (Major Hotel). What is the total cost of their stay?
    (A) £150
    (B) £160
    (C) £170
    (D) £180
    (E) £190

19 Which hotels are the cheapest for two and for four nights?
    (A) St Ives (Kings Hotel) and Bexhill (Eddy's Hotel)
    (B) Eastbourne (Prior Hotel) and Brighton (Bains Hotel)
    (C) Newquay (Major Hotel) and Brighton (Bains Hotel)
    (D) Eastbourne (Prior Hotel) and Bexhill (Eddy's Hotel)
    (E) Brighton (Dune Roaming Hotel) and St Ives (Kings Hotel)

20) Brighton (Bains Hotel) starts a promotion offering a 20% reduction for a two-night stay. What is the new cost of a two-night stay?
    (A) £88
    (B) £90
    (C) £98
    (D) £100
    (E) £108

Use the table of minimum and maximum temperatures to answer questions 21–25.

Minimum and maximum temperatures in five cities

Location	Minimum temperature (in centigrade)	Maximum temperature (in centigrade)	Maximum temperature (in Fahrenheit)
Lisbon	15	24	75
Madrid	12	25	77
Athens	22	28	82
London	13	15	59
Cardiff	14	17	63

21 Which two cities have the highest and the lowest temperatures?
(A) Athens and Cardiff
(B) Lisbon and Madrid
(C) Athens and Madrid
(D) Lisbon and Cardiff
(E) Lisbon and London

22 Which city has the greatest difference between the minimum and the maximum temperatures?
(A) Lisbon
(B) Madrid
(C) Athens
(D) London
(E) Cardiff

23 What is the range of maximum temperatures across the cities shown (in Fahrenheit)?
(A) 59–82
(B) 63–82
(C) 17–28
(D) 15–25
(E) 15–28

24 Which city has the highest maximum temperature (in Fahrenheit)?
(A) Lisbon

(B) Madrid

(C) Athens

(D) London

(E) Cardiff

25 Which two cities have maximum temperatures below 20 degrees centigrade?

(A) Athens and Cardiff

(B) Lisbon and Madrid

(C) Athens and Madrid

(D) Madrid and Cardiff

(E) Cardiff and London

The answers to these questions are on pages 117–18

The Army Entrance Tests – BARB answers

Question number	Largest number	Smallest number	Furthest away from third number	Answer option and answer
1 (the worked example)	8	1	$5 - 1 = 4$	(A) 1
2	9	3	$9 - 5 = 4$	(B) 9
3	7	1	$5 - 1 = 4$	(C) 1
4	12	6	$12 - 7 = 5$	(B) 12
5	9	1	$6 - 1 = 5$	(C) 1
6	14	8	$14 - 8 = 6$	(B) 14
7	16	9	$16 - 12 = 4$	(A) 16
8	18	1	$18 - 8 = 10$	(B) 18
9	19	8	$19 - 13 = 6$	(A) 19
10	12	7	$12 - 9 = 3$	(B) 12
11	8	3	$6 - 3 = 3$	(A) 3
12	12	3	$12 - 5 = 7$	(A) 12
13	11	5	$9 - 5 = 4$	(B) 5
14	7	1	$5 - 1 = 4$	(C) 1
15	15	2	$15 - 7 = 8$	(A) 15
16	17	2	$10 - 2 = 8$	(A) 2
17	16	3	$11 - 3 = 8$	(A) 3
18	17	8	$17 - 9 = 8$	(B) 17
19	19	9	$19 - 12 = 7$	(B) 19
20	18	3	$18 - 8 = 10$	(C) 18
21	12	1	$12 - 6 = 6$	(A) 12
22	11	5	$11 - 7 = 4$	(B) 11
23	14	2	$9 - 2 = 7$	(A) 2
24	16	3	$16 - 8 = 8$	(B) 16
25	20	2	$12 - 2 = 10$	(A) 2

Navy – Reasoning RT answers

1   The sequence 11, 9, 7, 5, 3 ... follows the pattern of sub-
     traction of 2 each time. Hence the answer is $3 - 2 = 1$.
     (A) 1

2   The sequence 5, 20, 35, 50, 65, 80 ... follows the pattern of
     the addition of 15 each time. Hence the answer is $80 + 15$
     $= 95$.
     (E) 95

3   The sequence 4, 8, 16, 32, 64 ... follows the pattern of mul-
     tiplication by 2 each time. Hence the answer is $64 \times 2 = 128$.
     (C) 128

4   The sequence 3, 6, 9, 12, 15 ... follows the pattern of the
     addition of 3 each time. Hence the answer is $15 + 3 = 18$.
     (C) 18

5   The sequence 5, 10, 15, 20, 25 ... follows the pattern of the
     addition of 5 each time. Hence the answer is $25 + 5 = 30$.
     (E) 30

6   The sequence 90, 77, 64, 51, 38 ... follows the pattern of
     the subtraction of 13 each time. Hence the answer is $38 -$
     $13 = 25$.
     (A) 25

7   The sequence 21, 36, 51, 66, 81 ... follows the pattern of
     the addition of 15 each time. Hence the answer is $81 + 15$
     $= 96$.
     (D) 96

8   The sequence 83, 71, 59, 47, 35 ... follows the pattern of
     the subtraction of 12 each time. Hence the answer is $35 -$
     $12 = 23$.
     (C) 23

9   The sequence of numbers 5, 10, 17, 26, 37 follows the

pattern of the addition of 5, then the addition of (5 + 2 = 7), then the addition of (7 + 2 = 9) and so on. Hence the answer is the next number in the series to add to 37, i.e. 37 + the addition of (11 + 2 = 13) = 37 + 13 = 50.

(E) 50

10 The sequence of numbers 2, 7, 4, 8, 6, 9 ... follows the pattern of two number series. The first number series, starting with the first number 2, is the addition of 2 each time (2 + 2 = 4; 4 + 2 = 6 and so on). The second number series, starting with the second number 7, is the addition of 1 each time (7 + 1 = 8; 8 + 1 = 9 and so on). Hence the answer – as part of the first series – is 6 + 2 = 8.

(B) 8

11 The sequence of numbers 36, 48, 60, 72, 84 ... follows the pattern of the addition of 12 each time. Hence the answer is 84 + 12 = 96.

(A) 96

12 The sequence of numbers 5, 3, 20, 6, 35, 9, 50 ... follows the pattern of two number series. The first number series, starting with the first number 5, is the addition of 15 each time (5 + 15 = 20; 20 + 15 = 35 and so on). The second number series, starting with the second number 3, is the addition of 3 each time (3 + 3 = 6; 6 + 3 = 9 and so on). Hence the answer – as part of the second series – is 9 + 3 = 12.

(E) 12

13 The sequence of numbers 25, 23, 20, 16, 11 ... follows the pattern of subtraction of 2, then subtraction of 3, then subtraction of 4, subtraction of 5 and so on. Hence the answer is the next in the sequence and so on which is subtraction by 6, i.e. 11 − 6 = 5.

(E) 5

14 The sequence of numbers 24, 33, 42, 51, 60 . . . follows the pattern of the addition of 9 each time. Hence the answer is 60 + 9 = 69.

(D) 69

15 The sequence of numbers 3, 5, 6, 10, 9, 20 . . . follows the pattern of two number series. The first number series, starting with the first number 3, is the addition of 3 each time (3 + 3 = 6; 6 + 3 = 9 and so on). The second number series, starting with the second number 5, is the multiplication by 2 each time (5 × 2 =10; 10 × 2 = 20 and so on). Hence the answer – as part of the first series – is 9 + 3 = 12.

(B) 12

16 The sequence of numbers 1, 2, 6, 24, 120 . . . follows the pattern of multiplication by 2, multiplication by 3, multiplication by 4, and multiplication by 5. Hence the answer is the next in the series: multiplication by 6 = 120 × 6 = 720.

(A) 720

17 The sequence of numbers 1, 2, 5, 14, 41 . . . follows the pattern of multiplication by 3 followed by subtraction of 1 (starting with 1 × 3 = 3; 3 − 1 = 2). Hence the answer is 41 × 3 = 123; 123 − 1 = 122.

(E) 122

18 The sequence of numbers 12, 3, 15, 7, 18, 11 . . . follows the pattern of two number series. The first number series, starting with the first number 12, is the addition of 3 each time (12 + 3 = 15; 15 + 3 = 18 and so on). The second number series, starting with the second number 25, is the addition of 4 each time (3 + 4 = 7; 7 + 4 = 11 and so on). Hence the answer – as part of the first series – is 18 + 3 = 21.

(B) 21

19 The sequence of numbers 201, 30, 191, 40, 181, 50 ... follows the pattern of two number series. The first number series, starting with the first number 201, is the subtraction of 10 each time (201 − 10 = 191; 191 − 10 = 181 and so on). The second number series, starting with the second number 30, is the addition of 10 each time (30 + 10 = 40; 40 + 10 = 50 and so on). Hence the answer – as part of the first series – is 181 − 10 = 171.

(C) 171

20 The sequence of numbers 1, 5, 25, 125 ... follows the pattern of multiplication by 5. Hence the answer is 125 × 5 = 625.

(E) 625

21 The sequence of numbers 2, 20, 38, 56 ... follows the pattern of the addition of 18 each time. Hence the answer is 56 + 18 = 74.

(B) 74

22 The sequence of numbers 2, 7, 13, 20, 28 ... follows the pattern of addition of 5, addition of 6, addition of 7, and addition of 8. Hence the answer is the next in the series, which is addition of 9, i.e. 28 + 9 = 37.

(D) 37

23 The sequence of numbers 4, 10, 5, 9, 6, 8 ... follows the pattern of two number series. The first number series, starting with the first number 4, is the addition of 1 each time (4 + 1 = 5; 5 + 1 = 6 and so on). The second number series, starting with the second number 10, is the subtraction of 1 each time (10 − 1 = 9; 9 − 1 = 8 and so on). Hence the answer – as part of the first series – is 6 + 1 = 7.

(E) 7

24 The sequence of numbers 2, 4, 10, 28, 82 ... follows the pattern of multiplication by 3, followed by subtraction of 2 (starting with $2 \times 3 = 6 - 2 = 4$). Hence the answer is 82 $\times 3 = 246; 246 - 2 = 244$.
(A) 244

25 The sequence of numbers 9, 25, 7, 30, 5, 35 ... follows the pattern of two number series. The first number series, starting with the first number 9, is the subtraction of 2 each time ($9 - 2 = 7; 7 - 2 = 5$ and so on). The second number series, starting with the second number 25, is the addition of 5 each time ($25 + 5 = 30; 30 + 5 = 35$ and so on). Hence the answer – as part of the first series – is $5 - 2 = 3$.
(E) 3

Navy – Numeracy RT answers

1   (D) 55.37
Step 1 – Review the third figure after the decimal point
This is greater than 5 so the second figure after the decimal point needs to be rounded up

2   (C) 9778

3   (A) 2000
$5,000 \times 40 / 100 = 2000$

4   (D) 300 square metres
20 metres $\times$ 15 metres = 300 square metres

5   (B) 45.8

6   (E) 40%
$100 \times 0.4 / 1 = 40\%$

7   (A) £8.75
£50.00 $\times$ 17.5 / 100 = £8.75

8   (C) 231

9   (B) £810
Step 1 – Total budget calculation
9 × average utilities bill = 9 × £90 = £810

10   (C) 200
500 × 40 / 100 = 200

11   (E) 0.65

12   (D) 50 miles per hour
Step 1 – Calculate the time taken
11.00 hrs − 09.00 hrs represents 2 hours
Step 2 – Average speed calculation
Average speed = distance / time taken = 100 miles / 2 hours
= 50 mph

13   (B) 15.684
Step 1 – Review fourth decimal place
Fourth decimal place is less than 5 so the third figure after
the decimal point needs to be rounded down

14   (C) ⅖

15   (A) 50

16   (E) ¹⁄₂₄
⅓ × ⅛ = 1/ (3×8) = ¹⁄₂₄

17   (C) 0.7
70/100 = 0.7

18   (D) ¹⁄₁₀

19   C = 32,800

20   A = 38 hours
Step 1 – Calculate the hours during the week
7 × 5 = 35 hours
Step 2 – Add weekend hours
Total hours = 35 + 3 = 38 hours

RAF 1 answers

1   (C) $50 \times 0.5 = 25$

2   (D) $0.98 + 0.47 = 1.45$

3   (A) $432 + 88 = 520$

4   (B) $12 \times 200 = 2{,}400$

5   (D) $0.66 - 0.23 = 0.43$

6   (A) $\frac{1}{3} \times 33 = 11$

7   (D) $225 - 44 = 181$

8   (C) $0.5 \times 36 = 18$

9   (B) $15 \times \frac{1}{3} = 5$

10   (E) $0.45 \times 200 = 90$

11   (C) 31.456 expressed to two decimal places $= 31.46$

12   (C) $\frac{1}{3} + \frac{1}{2} = \frac{5}{6}$

13   (D) $46 / 4.6 = 10$

14   (B) $\frac{1}{4} \times 600 = 150$

15   (B) $0.25 \times 0.5 = 0.125$

16   (C) $90 + 0.99 = 90.99$

17   (A) $550 / 11 = 50$

18   (C) $5.5 \times 9.5 = 52.25$

19   (A) $\frac{1}{4} \times 500 = 125$

20   (D) 30% of $250 = 75$

RAF 2 answers

1   (D) £7.77

2   (E) £3.30

3   (A) 60p more

4   (B) 2

5   (B) Bag of crisps and greetings card

6   (D) Milk

7   (C) £1.12

8   (B) Fruit, meat and cheese

9   (E) Fruit and cheese

10   (A) £2.50

11   (B) Belgium and Denmark

12   (E) Belgium and Germany

13   (D) 50

14   (C) 340

15   (E) 140

16   (C) £349

17   (E) £350

18   (D) £180

19 (D) Eastbourne (Prior Hotel) and Bexhill (Eddy's Hotel)

20 (A) £88

21 (C) Athens and Madrid

22 (B) Madrid

23 (A) 59–82

24 (C) Athens

25 (E) Cardiff and London

✷ brilliant warning

Read the question carefully. Double check what the question asks for if you need to.

● Question 11 asks 'Which countries have the highest and the lowest confectionery imports?' Do not answer with one of the distracter options.

● Question 17 specifically states 'A couple'.

● Question 23 specifically asks 'What is the range of maximum temperatures across the cities shown (in Fahrenheit)?'

CHAPTER 7

Qualified Teacher Status: Numeracy Skills Test

I n order to become a qualified teacher in England, trainees must take three computerised tests in literacy, numeracy and ICT. Passing all three tests is a prerequisite for attaining the Qualified Teacher Status (QTS) needed to teach at a maintained school (or a non-maintained school as a qualified teacher). You might be wondering why you need to take a numeracy test if you don't intend to specialise in mathematics. The reason is to ensure that *all* teachers, regardless of their subject, have the necessary level of numerical ability to carry out their professional duties – which range from scoring exams to interpreting educational reports and balancing budgets.

How is it taken?

For security and confidentiality reasons you can't take the test from the comfort of your own home. Instead, the test is taken online under supervised test conditions at a test centre. The three tests can be taken altogether in one sitting or one at a time. There are approximately fifty QTS Skills Test Centres around the country, at locations such as schools, universities and further education colleges, as well as commercial test centres.

What is the pass mark?

There are 28 available marks on the numeracy test – one per question. The numeracy test has been benchmarked. This means that there are slight variations in difficulty depending on which test is given. Thus the pass mark varies a bit – it is lower for a test with slightly harder questions and higher for a test with slightly easier questions. That said, the pass mark is a minimum of 60% for the numeracy test – or 17 marks out of the 28 available. Your result will be given to you at the end of the day. Fear not – if you do not pass on your first attempt, the QTS tests can be retaken.

What does it test?

The QTS Numeracy test is designed to ensure that teachers have a foundation in the basic applications of numeracy *within the teaching profession*. The content of the questions is education-specific, so you will be tested on applying the numeracy skills that are needed in the classroom. This is a very practically focused test and is divided into two sets of questions. It begins with an audio test of mental arithmetic questions. The second part of the test involves answering on-screen questions involving the interpretation of statistical information and the use of general arithmetic. In total, the test will take 48 minutes. This chapter deals firstly with the mental arithmetic section and then covers the on-screen questions.

 **resources**

Many of the QTS Skills Test Centres are listed on the internet, including details of how to book and what information to take along on the testing day. You can find additional information about the test by visiting:

http://www.tda.gov.uk/skillstests.aspx

Search the Government's Directgov website for useful information on the role of a teacher, as well as the qualifications required and how to apply.

Search for specific teaching roles at:

http://careersadvice.direct.gov.uk/helpwithyourcareer/jobprofiles/

Mental arithmetic

The first set of mental arithmetic questions test the numerical reasoning skills that a newly qualified teacher would be expected to demonstrate every day. During this portion of the QTS skills test you listen to the mental arithmetic questions using headphones and must answer them without a calculator. You cannot move forwards or backwards between questions in this test.

The mental arithmetic questions cover the following areas:

- fractions;
- ratios;
- percentages;
- converting between all of the above (percentages, fractions and ratios);
- decimal points;
- measurements, e.g. metres (for distance), cubic centimetres (for volume), square metres (for area);
- the 24-hour clock;
- pounds sterling and other currencies, i.e. using exchange rates effectively;
- statistical averages, including means, modes, medians, range, quartile range;
- simple formulae, i.e. dropping the right figures into a formula supplied by the question.

Instructions

Listen to the questions through the headphones. Each question is repeated. There is then a pause during which you are expected to type in your answer. When this time is up – or if you selected to move on prior to this – the next question appears. You have one practice question before the test starts.

Listening to audio questions is different from seeing the information immediately presented to you on a page. But just think of this as one extra stage. You need to listen carefully and, on the rough paper provided, write down all the numerical information for that question. This is your priority. The question will be repeated so you don't need to write everything down in a rush. If you miss one of the figures focus on writing this down the second time that you hear the question. Only then should you carry out the calculation alongside the question that you have written down.

Even if you are very nervous on the day, make sure that you at the very least write the question down. Remember, once you have written all the numbers down you just need to work out the calculation as you normally would.

brilliant tips

- Some of the questions will involve a simple multiplication or percentage calculation. For other questions you may need to write down three or four key figures.
- When asked to provide fractions in the lowest terms remember to divide these by the highest common denominator – also known as the highest common factor.

Practice questions

1   There are 15 boys and 10 girls in a class. What is the ratio of girls to boys?

2   A school trip is planned. Parents are asked to pay 90% of the total cost. If the total cost is £55.50 how much must the parents pay in total?

3   School lunch break is scheduled for 12.30 hrs. There are 3

classes lasting 65 minutes each prior to this lunch break. At what time do classes start?

4   A child walks 1.25 km to school. If the child walks on average at 5 km per hour, how long does this journey take?

5   A small class of pupils achieves the following marks on a test: 6, 8, 9, 10, 12, 10, 8. What is the mean score?

6   A parent gives her son £6.00 spending money for a school day trip to France. If the exchange rate is 1.2 Euros to the £, how many Euros equivalent does the parent give her son?

7   A class is comprised of three fifths girls. If there are 20 children in the class, what are the numbers of boys and girls?

8   The cost for a pair of school uniform trousers is £14.99 in the local suppliers. What would be the cost for two siblings including a spare pair?

9   The afternoon break has been delayed by 40 minutes for a teacher emergency. If the usual time for afternoon break is 14.25 hrs, what time is the delayed afternoon break?

10   In a spelling test of 20 questions, pupils score the following range of results: 9, 11, 5, 16, 15, 20, 18, 14 and 17. What is the median?

11   The head teacher took part in a sponsored swim for charity. Sixty-three pupils sponsored the head teacher at an average of 5p per length. If the head teacher swam 50 lengths, how much money was raised in sponsorship?

12   The highest mark achieved in a test was 16 out of 25. What is this expressed as a percentage?

13   What is ¼ multiplied by ⅓?

14   The school is selling two sets of raffle tickets. A parent buys

5 tickets at 75p each and 8 tickets at 50p each. How much change does the parent get from £10.00?

15   What is 3.2 multiplied by 50?

16   The school coach travels 45 miles to the school and then 45 miles back to the depot. How much petrol (in litres) does the coach use on a typical round trip if it travels an average of 8 miles per litre?

17   To obtain an A-grade pupils needed to get 15 or above in a test. The scores were 10, 15, 16, 12, 20, 19, 18, 9, 15 and 14. What percentage of pupils got an A grade?

18   What is 0.9×0.5?

19   A school day lasts for seven and a quarter hours. If school starts at 09.00 hrs, what time does school finish (using the 24-hour clock)?

20   Out of a year group of 84 pupils, 25% achieved Key Stage 3. How many pupils does this represent?

21   One eighth of pupils at a school receive free school meals. What percentage is this?

22   Twenty of a school's 130 pupils are in the school choir. What fraction of pupils are in the school choir?

23   Fifteen pupils paid £9.50 for a school trip to a museum. On average each pupil spent an additional £3.25 in the museum shop. What was the total amount spent by the 15 pupils?

24   On an exchange trip to Germany, one pupil gave €5 to his friend to spend, gave €7 to his sister and spent €14 himself. At an exchange rate of 1.25 Euros to the £ how much did he spend (in £)?

25   In a class of 30 pupils, 12 are boys. What fraction of the class are girls?

26 A school trip to see a play costs £5.50 for the coach travel and £12.75 for the ticket. If a parent wants to allow their two children to each have £2.00 to spend on refreshments, what will the total cost be?

27 On the last day of term school finishes 90 minutes early. If the usual finish time is 15.15 hrs, what time does school finish on the last day of term?

28 A 1.5 km school walk is planned. What is this distance in miles (using the conversion 1 km : 0.6 mile)?

29 A small class of pupils achieves the following marks on a test: 14, 16, 18, 19, 20, 15, 20 and 18. What is the mean score?

30 A coffee morning to raise money for the school sells teas for 35p, coffees for 50p and biscuits for 20p. Thirty teas, 40 coffees and 50 biscuits are sold. What is the total amount raised?

31 What is 0.45×8?

32 30% of a class of 40 receive free school meals. How many pupils does this represent?

33 One fifth of pupils at a school walk to school. What percentage is this?

34 A school has 115 pupils; 20% of these take dance class on a Monday. How many pupils take dance class?

35 The return journey to school costs £2.50 by bus. How much would be saved each week by walking to school?

36 A visitor gives a class talk lasting for an hour and a quarter. If the class starts at 12.30 hrs, what time does the talk finish (using the 24-hour clock)?

37 In a spelling test of 30 questions, pupils score the following

range of results: 19, 21, 15, 26, 25, 30, 28, 24 and 27. What is the median?

38   What is ⅚ as a percentage?

39   What is ½ × ½?

40   The annual school fete raises £2,051.00. The book stall raises £615.30. What is this as a percentage of the total amount raised?

41   Afternoon classes last three hours. If afternoon classes finish at 15.30 hrs, what time do afternoon classes start?

42   In a trip to the local swimming pool the teacher is required to collect £2.75 from each of her 12 pupils. Three pupils have not brought the entrance charge to the local leisure centre with them. How much money does the teacher collect?

43   In a sponsored running race four teachers raise £24.33, £19.90, £15.75 and £46.80 respectively. How much money is raised in total?

44   What is 40% of 680?

45   A school's attendance rate drops by a tenth over a term. If the rate was 90% at the start of term, what is the attendance rate (in %) at the end of term?

46   The school notice board measures 2 metres by 2 metres. What is the area of the school notice board?

47   A school has 220 pupils; 55 pupils take gymnastics lessons on Saturday mornings. What percentage of the school pupils take gymnastics lessons?

48   As part of a lesson 17 pupils are asked to each read aloud for 5 minutes. If the class starts at 11.20 hrs, what time does the class finish?

49 A quarter of a class go to the school playing fields whilst the remainder play in the playground. If there are 28 pupils in the class, how many pupils play in the playground?

50 What is 0.54×3?

On-screen questions

The second part of the QTS numeracy test is considerably more difficult than the mental arithmetic questions. An on-screen calculator is provided for answering the questions and this time you have a set time for answering *all* the questions. More complex numeracy skills are being tested *in addition* to all the mathematical operations from the first part of the test. This portion of the test is designed to assess:

● analysing trends in sets of figures, e.g. from one year to the next;

● making comparisons between one or more sets of data, e.g. different test results;

● interpreting figures contained in tables, charts and graphs (histograms, pie charts, scatter plots, line graphs).

The on-screen questions are set in the context of the teaching profession: setting test targets, meeting national standards and the monitoring of pupil-related data, such as gender and class sizes. The questions assess whether a trainee possesses the core numerical skills essential for fulfilling their professional role in the school.

So many different types of question can be found in the on-screen test that it is not possible to cover the full range. This is mainly because of the sheer extent of school data and the variety of ways that such statistical data can be represented in graphs. On some of the examples that I have given you could be asked to apply other numerical reasoning skills and to interpret more complex questions.

To further prepare you, I have listed most of these below:

- Algebra
  You may be asked to plug numbers into an algebraic formula. For example, using an algebra equation to convert distance from miles to kilometres or temperature from Fahrenheit to Celsius.

- Weighting
  More difficult questions might involve calculating weighted test scores using a formula. Any such equation will be given to you in the question.

- Cumulative frequency tables and graphs
  For example, adding the number of pupils who achieved Level 2 to those who achieved Level 3, then adding this running total to those pupils who achieved Level 4, and so on.

- Medians, means and modes
  You need to know how to interpret median, means and modes from graphical formats such as cumulative frequency graphs.

- Box and whisker plots
  For example, a box and whisker plot may ask you for the interquartile range, the upper quartile, the lower quartile, the minimum, the maximum and/or the range of scores.

Instructions

In addition to selecting the correct multiple choice answer option there are a few things you need to know about answering the on-screen questions. It's easy enough and certainly nothing to worry about. Just don't be surprised when the question asks you to answer in a different way than you expected.

For some questions you will just type in your multiple choice selection, but for other questions you may have to do one of the following:

- Type in your actual answer. Type in only the figures – you do not need to show the units of measurement.

- Highlight with the cursor or mouse more than one *True* statement from a list of statements.

- Drag and drop your answer, for example to fill in a missing box in a table.

- Highlight the correct answer by clicking with the cursor or mouse. For example, showing a point on a graph that you have been asked to recognise.

Unlike the audio part of the test, this time you can scroll backwards and forwards between the questions. This allows you to work at your own pace. After answering the last question you will be asked if you want to review any questions that you have 'flagged' by pressing the *Flag* button. Take advantage of being able to move forwards and backwards by completing the easiest questions first. If any time remains at the end, go back and enter answers for any questions that you missed out.

You will see a clock displayed on the computer screen. Keep a firm eye on this throughout the test! The test ends automatically when the time limit expires.

There is more information to take in with the on-screen questions. Make sure that you are clear about anything that is required beyond the calculation. For example, does it ask you to round it up or down to the nearest decimal place? Do you need to convert the table or graph data into a percentage?

Ensure that you fully comprehend the layout of any table or graph. Spending more time than is necessary on the first question pays off as you will save time on subsequent questions based on the same numerical information.

Practice questions

1   The school trip to the Christmas ice-skating rink costs £3.75 entrance per pupil. There is a 5% reduction in the entrance fee for booking in advance. How much would be saved by booking in advance for 53 pupils?

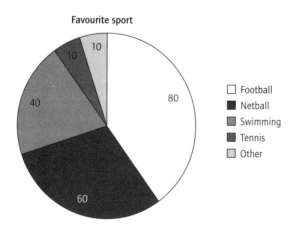

Favourite sport

2   In a school survey each of the pupils was asked what their favourite sport was. The pie chart shows the pupils' results. Indicate all the true statements:

a) There are 200 pupils in total at the school.
b) For a quarter of the pupils swimming is their favourite sport.
c) 40% of the school pupils chose football as their favourite sport.

Percentage of male pupils passing a Maths test (compared to the national average)

	2006	2007	2008
Boy pupils (%)	80	99.2	98.2
National average (%)	51.2	51.2	51.2

Use the table showing the *Percentage of male pupils passing a Maths test (compared to the national average)* to answer question 3.

3   Indicate all the true statements:
a) The % of boys passing the Maths tests has been higher than the national average each year between 2006 and 2008.
b) The national average on the Maths test has improved each year between 2006 and 2008.
c) The % of boys passing the test has increased between 2007 and 2008.

Primary school's attendance figures (compared to the national average)

	Attendance rate 2003/04	Attendance rate 2004/05	Attendance rate 2005/06
School (%)	94.9	94.7	94.9
National average (%)	94.7	94.9	95.1

Use the table showing *Primary school's attendance figures (compared to the national average)* to answer question 4.

4   Indicate all the true statements:
a) The school's attendance rate increased between 2003 and 2006.

b) The national average has consistently decreased each year.

c) For school year 2004/05 the school's attendance rate was below that of the national average.

5   The new head teacher is planning the Easter play that the school is putting on. She wants to start the performance one and a half hours after school finishes at 15.50. The head teacher also wants to allow 15 minutes after arrival time for parents to mingle. The play lasts 35 minutes. What time will it finish? Give your answer using the 24-hour clock.

GCSE subjects taken by secondary school pupils for first Monday morning lesson

GCSE subject	Number of secondary pupils
Maths	60
Chemistry	28
Physics	33
Biology	34
History	28
Geography	22
French	19
English	56
Computing	36
Geography	14

To answer questions 6 and 7 use the table *GCSE subjects taken by secondary school pupils for first Monday morning lesson*.

6   What percentage of pupils has Maths as their first lesson on a Monday morning? Give your answer to one decimal place.

7   What fraction of pupils has Physics as their first lesson on a Monday morning?

Pupil scores on two Maths tests

	Maths test A (out of 25)	Maths test B (out of 30)
Girl 1	19	22
Girl 2	15	25
Girl 3	11	19
Girl 4	25	27
Girl 5	22	20
Girl 6	18	22

To answer question 8 use the table *Pupil scores on two Maths tests.*

8   Indicate all the true statements:
   a) The score ranges for Maths tests A and B are 11–26 and 19–27.
   b) The mean scores for Maths tests A and B are 18.3 and 22.5 (to one decimal place).
   c) The mode for Maths test B is 22.

Number of primary school pupils 2006–08 compared to the national average

	2006	2007	2008
School pupils	185	174	165
National average	242	240	241

Use the table showing *Number of primary school pupils 2006–08 (compared to the national average)* to answer question 9.

9   Which year had the highest school size as a percentage of the national average?

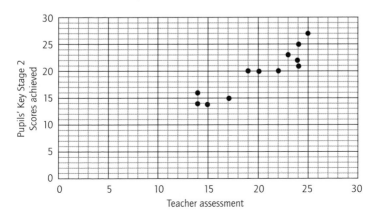

Use the previous scatter plot of *Pupils' Key Stage 2 scores compared to teacher assessment* to answer questions 10 and 11.

10   How many pupils performed at or above the teacher's assessment?

11   What was the mean score achieved? Give your answer correct to one decimal place.

Use the table showing the *Number of pupils achieving A-level passes* to answer question 12.

Number of pupils achieving A-level passes

A-level passes	1	2	3	4
Number of pupils	5	29	49	15

12   What percentage of pupils achieved fewer than three A-level passes? Give your answer to the nearest whole percentage.

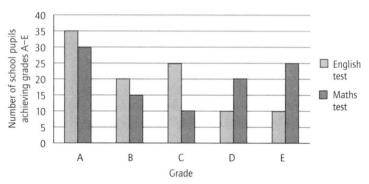

To answer question 13 use the graph *English and Maths test grades for 100 pupils*.

13   Indicate all the true statements:
    a) Overall performance was higher in the English test compared to the Maths test.
    b) 55% of pupils got an A or B grade in the English test.
    c) Less than half the pupils got grades C, D or E in the Maths test.

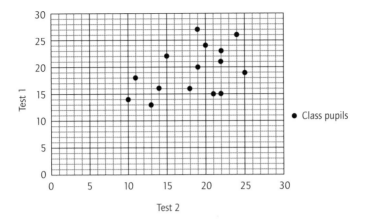

Use the previous scatter plot showing *Test 1 compared to Test 2 scores for class pupils* to answer question 14.

14 Indicate all the true statements:

a) A third of the class pupils scored lower marks on Test 2 compared to Test 1.

b) The score range for Test 1 differs from the score range for Test 2.

c) The pupil with the lowest score on Test 2 scored the lowest score on Test 1.

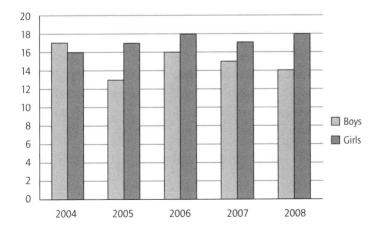

To answer question 15 refer to the previous graph *Pupil genders of class 2004–2008.*

15 Indicate all the true statements:
   a) The number of boys by year ranges from 13 to 17.
   b) The smallest class size was in year 2007.
   c) There have been more girls than boys in the class each year between 2004 and 2008.

Boy and girl spelling test scores (out of 20)

Girls	Spelling test results	Boys	Spelling test results
Girl 1	14	Boy 1	18
Girl 2	16	Boy 2	12
Girl 3	12	Boy 3	13
Girl 4	11	Boy 4	19
Girl 5	19	Boy 5	14
Girl 6	17	Boy 6	12
Girl 7	9	Boy 7	18

To answer question 16 refer to the table *Boy and girl spelling test scores (out of 20).*

16 Indicate all the true statements:
   a) The mean score for all boys and girls was 16.
   b) Boys had a smaller range of scores than girls.
   c) The median test score for girls was 12.

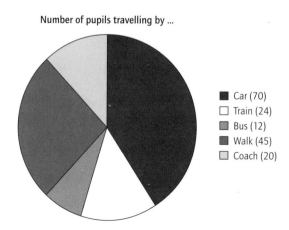

Number of pupils travelling by ...

- Car (70)
- Train (24)
- Bus (12)
- Walk (45)
- Coach (20)

To answer question 17 refer to the pie-chart showing *Number of pupils travelling to school by different forms of transport.*

17 Indicate all the true statements:
   a) More than twice as many pupils walk compared to those who travel by coach.
   b) The ratio of those who travel by train compared to those who walk is 1 : 2.
   c) Less than half the pupils travel to school by car.

Pupil numbers taking Thursday drama lessons

Term	Number of pupils taking drama lessons each week
Winter term	16–25
Spring term	19–30
Summer term	18–22

To answer question 18 use the table *Pupil numbers taking Thursday drama lessons.*

18 What was the range in pupil numbers across all three terms?

Pupils attaining Levels 2 and 3 in Key Stage 1 tests for English and Maths

	English	Maths
Level 2 – Boys	28	22
Level 2 – Girls	26	25
Level 3 – Boys	11	10
Level 3 – Girls	12	14

To answer question 19 use the table of *Pupils attaining Levels 2 and 3 in Key Stage 1 tests for English and Maths.*

19 Indicate all the true statements:
   a) Less than a third of the pupils who took the Maths test achieved Level 3.
   b) More than 70% of the pupils who took the English test achieved Level 2.
   c) More girls than boys achieved Level 2 in the English test.

Mean scores from a standardised reading test results for 7+ pupils

	Class size	Reading test standardised score 7+
Class 1	30	15
Class 2	29	20
Class 3	31	16

Use the table *Mean scores from a standardised reading test results for 7+ pupils* to answer question 20.

20   What is the mean for all three classes? Give your answer to one decimal place.

brilliant resources

You can download excellent sample practice questions from the Training and Development Agency for Schools' website.

http://www.tda.gov.uk/skillstests/numeracy/practicematerials.aspx

The BBC's Skillswise site has some basic guidance on areas such as fractions, percentages, decimals, handling graphical data and measuring distance, size and weight.

http://www.bbc.co.uk/skillswise

QTS Mental arithmetic answers

1   2 : 3
      Step 1 – Put the totals for each gender into a ratio
      10 : 15
      Step 2 – Simplify the ratio by dividing by the highest common denominator
      Highest common denominator = 5
      10/5 : 15/5
      This ratio simplifies to 2 : 3

2   £49.95
Calculate 90% of £55.50
£55.50 × 90 / 100 = £49.95

3   09.15 hrs
Step 1 – Calculate the total length of the 3 classes
65 × 3 = 195 minutes
Step 2 – Calculate this in hours
195 / 60 = 3 hours and 15 mins
Step 3 – Work backwards by deducting 3 hours and 15 mins
from 12.30
12.30 hrs − 3 hours and 15 mins = 09.15 hrs

4   15 minutes
Apply the equation *Speed = Distance/Time*
5 km/h = 1.25 km/time
Time = 1.25 / 5 = ¼ of an hour
¼ of an hour = 15 minutes

5   9
Step 1 – Calculate the sum of the scores
6 + 8 + 9 + 10 + 12 + 10 + 8 = 63
Step 2 – Calculate the mean by dividing this sum by the
number of pupil scores
63 / 7 = 9

6   €7.2
Apply the exchange rate
6 × 1.2 = €7.2

7   8 boys, 12 girls
Step 1 – Calculate how many girls
20 × ⅗ = 12 girls
Step 2 – Calculate how many boys
20 − 12 = 8 boys

8   £44.97
Calculate the cost for three sets of trousers
£14.99 × 3 = £44.97

9   15.05 hrs

Add on 40 minutes to 14.25 hrs

14.25 hrs + 40 minutes = 14.65 hrs

However . . .

. . . a new hour starts after 60 minutes. Thus the delayed time is 15.05 hrs

10   15

Calculate the middle or median value by putting the scores in order

5, 9, 11, 14, 15, 16, 17, 18, 20

The middle score when there are nine scores is the fifth score, i.e. 15

11   £157.50

Step 1 – Calculate the average cost per pupil

5p × 50 = £2.50

Step 2 – Multiply the cost per pupil by the number of pupils

£2.50 × 63 = £157.50

12   64%

100 × 16/25 = 64%

13 $\frac{1}{12}$

14   £2.25

Step 1 – Calculate the total cost

(75 × 5) + (50 × 8) = 775p = £7.75

Step 2 – Deduct the total cost from £10.00

£10.00 − £7.75 = £2.25

15   160

16   11.25 litres

Calculate the total distance travelled

45 miles × 2 = 90 miles

Step 2 – Calculate how much petrol is used over 90 miles

90/8 = 11.25 litres

17 60%

Step 1 – Calculate the number of pupils who got 15 or above

6 pupils (with scores of 15, 16, 20, 19, 18, 15)

Step 2 – Calculate the percentage of the total number of pupils

Total number of pupils = 10

$100 \times 6 / 10 = 60\%$

18 0.45

19 16.15 hrs

20 21

$84 \times 25 / 100 = 21$

21 12.5%

$100 \times 1/8 = 12.5\%$

22 $\frac{2}{13}$

$20/130 = 2/13$

23 £191.25

Step 1 – Calculate the total amount spent per pupil

£9.50 + £3.25 = £12.75

Step 2 – Multiply by 15 (pupils)

$15 \times £12.75 = £191.25$

24 £20.80

Step 1 – Sum the total amount spent

$5 + 7 + 14 = 26$

Step 2 – Apply the exchange rate

$26/1.25 = £20.80$

25 $\frac{3}{5}$

Step 1 – Calculate the number of girls

$30 - 12 = 18$

Step 2 – Calculate this as a fraction

$\frac{18}{30} = \frac{3}{5}$

26 £40.50
Step 1 – Sum the total costs per child
£5.50 + £12.75 + £2.00 = £20.25
Multiply by 2 for the two siblings
£20.25 × 2 = £40.50

27 13.45 hrs
90 minutes (1 hour and 30 minutes) before 15.15 hrs is 13.45 hrs

28 0.9 miles
1 km : 0.6 mile
1.5 × 0.6 = 0.9 miles

29 17.5
Step 1 – Calculate the total
14 + 16 + 18 + 19 + 20 + 15 + 20 + 18 = 140
Step 2 – Mean (the average) = Total / number of scores
140 / 8 = 17.5

30 £40.50
(30 × 35p) + (40 × 50p) + (50 × 20p) = £10.50 + £20.00 + £10.00 = £40.50

31 3.6

32 12
30 / 100 × 40 = 12

33 20%

34 23
115 × 20 / 100 = 23

35 £12.50
£2.50 × 5 = £12.50

36 13.45 hrs

37 25

Calculate the middle median value by putting the scores in order

15, 19, 21, 24, 25, 26, 27, 28, 30

The middle score when there are nine scores is the fifth score, i.e. 25

38 83.3%

5 / 6 × 100 = 83.3%

39 ¼

40 30%

100 × £615.30 / £2,051.00 = 30%

41 12.30 hrs

42 £24.75

9 × £2.75 = £24.75

43 £106.78

£24.33 + £19.90 + £15.75 + £46.80 = £106.78

44 272

45 81%

90 × 9/10 = 81%

46 4 square metres

47 25%

48 12.45 hrs

Step 1 – Calculate the time taken

17 × 5 minutes = 85 minutes

Step 2 – Add 85 minutes to 11.20 hrs

85 minutes = 1 hour 25 minutes, so the new time is 12.45 hrs

49 21

50 1.62

QTS On-screen answers

Question	Answer	Step 1	Step 2	Step 3
1	£188.81	£3.75 × 53 = £198.75	£198.75 × 5% = £9.94	
2	a is true c is true	Statement a is true. This is proved by adding up each part of the pie to get the total number of pupils, as follows: 80 + 60 + 40 + 10 + 10 = 200 Statement c is true. 80 of the 200 pupils chose football: 80 / 200 × 100% = 40% Statement b is false. This is demonstrated as follows; 40 pupils have swimming as their favourite sport. 40 / 200 = 1/5		
3	a is true	Statement a is true. For the dates 2006, 2007 and 2008 the percentage of boys passing the Maths test has been higher than the national average. Statement b is false since between dates 2006 and 2008 the national average has stayed the same at 51.2%. Statement c is false since between 2007 and 2008 the percentage of boys passing the test reduced from 99.2% to 98.2%.		
4	c is true	Statement a is false since the school's attendance rate decreased from 94.9% for school year 2003/04 to 94.7% for school year 2004/05. Statement b is false since the national trend has consistently increased – not decreased – between each set of school years shown. Statement c is true. This is proved by looking at the difference between the figures for attendance rate 2004/05 and the national average (94.9 − 94.7 = 0.2).		
5	18.10 hrs	Add one and a half hours to 15.50 hrs = 17.20 hrs	Add 15 minutes to 17.20 hrs = 17.35 hrs	Add 35 minutes to 17.35 hrs = 18.10 hrs
6	18.2%	There are 330 pupils in total	60 pupils have Maths	100 × 60/330 = 18.185 = 18.2% (to 1 decimal place)

Question	Answer	Step 1	Step 2	Step 3
7	$\frac{1}{10}$	33 pupils have Physics	$^{33}\!/_{330} = \frac{1}{10}$	
8	b is true c is true	Statement b is true because both mean scores are correct. Mean for Maths test A = $(19 + 15 + 11 + 25 + 22 + 18)$ / 6 = 18.3 Mean for Maths test B = $(22 + 25 + 19 + 27 + 20 + 22)$ / 6 = 22.5 Statement c is true. The mode for Maths test B is the most popular score which is 22. Statement a is false because the score range for Maths test A is 11–25 (not 11–26).		
9	2006	The percentage school size (against the national average) needs to be calculated for each year	2006; 185/242 $\times$ 100% = 76.4% 2007; 174/240 $\times$ 100% = 72.5% 2008;165/241 $\times$ 100% = 68.5%	The highest percentage school size (against the national average) was in 2006.
10	7	The scatter plot shows that 7 pupils had Score Achieved marks that were at or higher than their Teacher assessment mark.		
11	19.8	Mean score = $(27 + 25 + 23 + 22 + 21 + 20 + 20 + 20 + 16 + 15 + 14 + 14)/12$	Mean score = 19.75	19.8 (to one decimal place)
12	35%	Pupils achieving 2 A-level passes + Pupils achieving 1 A-level pass = 29 + 5 = 34	Total number of pupils = 5 + 29 + 49 + 15 = 98	34/98 $\times$ 100% = 34.69% 34.69% = 35% to the nearest %

Question	Answer	Step 1	Step 2	Step 3
13	a is true b is true	Statement a is true since overall performance was higher in the English test compared to the Maths test. More pupils achieved A and B grades on the English test. Fewer pupils received the lowest D and E grades. Statement b is true since 55% of pupils (35 + 20 = 55 out of 100 pupils) got an A or B grade in the English test. Statement c is false since more than half the pupils got grades C, D or E in the Maths test (10 + 20 + 25 = 55 out of 100 pupils).		
14	b is true	Statement a is false because more than a third of the class pupils scored lower marks on Test 2 compared to Test 1. Statement c is false because the pupil with the lowest score on Test 2 did not score the lowest score on Test 1. Statement b is true because the score range for Test 2 (25 − 10 = 15) differs from that for Test 1 (27 − 13 = 14).		
15	a is true	Statement a is true because the number of boys by year ranges from 13 to 17. The lowest point shown is 13. The highest point shown is 17. Statement b is false because the smallest class size was in year 2005 (30 pupils) and not in year 2007 (32 pupils). Statement c is false because in one year (2004) there were fewer girls than boys in the class.		
16	b is true	Statement a is false: Mean score = (total for boys and girls)/12 = 204/14 = 14.57 Statement b is true: Score range (Boys) = 12 to 19 = 7 Score range (Girls) = 9 to 19 = 10 Statement c is false because putting the female scores in the following order; 9, 11, 12, 14, 16, 17, 19 shows that the median score was 14.		

Question	Answer	Step 1	Step 2	Step 3
17	a is true c is true	Statement a is true because the 45 pupils who walk to school is over twice the number (20) of those who travel by coach.		
		Statement c is true because the 70 pupils who travel to school by car is less than half the total (Total number of pupils = 70 + 20 + 45 + 12 + 24 = 171).		
		Statement b is false because the ratio of those who travel by train compared to those who walk is not 1 : 2 but 24 : 45.		
18	16–30	The overall range is the lowest number of drama class pupils (16) to the highest number of drama class pupils (30).		
19	b is true	Statement a is false. Total pupils taking Maths test = 22 + 25 + 10 + 14 = 71 Total pupils achieving grade 3 = 10 + 14 = 24 $^{24}/_{71}$ is more than a third.		
		Statement b is true. Total pupils taking the English test = 28 + 24 + 11 + 12 = 75. Total pupils who achieved Level 2 = 28 + 26 = 54 100 × 54 / 75 = 72%		
		Statement c is false. Fewer girls than boys achieved Level 2 in the English test.		
20	17.0	(30 × 15) + (29 × 20) + (31 × 16)/(30 + 29 + 31) = 1526 / 90 = 16.955 = (17.0 to one decimal place)		

Additional answer explanations

I've pulled out three questions and provided a more detailed explanation of their answer below:

Question 3

Here you can see how percentages come into their own as one of the most effective ways of comparing figures. The graphs and tables in QTS demonstrate how certain sorts of data are best suited to particular graphical formats.

Question 10

Here you can see how scatter plots come into their own as one of the most effective ways of plotting two sets of scores and being able to clearly show overall performance for one set of scores compared to the other set of scores. Often a median line is plotted on such a scatter plot to split the top 50% (above the median line) from the bottom 50% (below the median line). You may also see the upper quartile and lower quartile lines plotted above and below this median line.

Question 12

It is important to be able to quickly round up your answer to the number of decimal places specified in the question. The key things to remember are first that this is the last part of your calculation. Secondly, you only need to remember that the cut-off is .5. Anything lower and you round down. Anything higher, or 5 itself, and you round up.

CHAPTER 8

UKCAT

ritish medical and dental schools are highly selective. Each year, an abundance of highly qualified candidates compete for a limited number of places on courses. This is why applicants to most British medical and dental schools will need to take the UK Clinical Aptitude Test for Medical and Dental Degrees (UKCAT). The test enables universities to select the most suitable candidates from a large pool of talented applicants. Rather than focusing on academic achievements, the UKCAT tests the general mental abilities needed to be a successful healthcare professional.

How is it taken?

The UKCAT Consortium of Medical and Dental Schools and Pearson VUE run the UKCAT test process. You attend one of Pearson VUE's test centres to take five multiple choice sub-tests:

1 Verbal Reasoning;

2 Quantitative Reasoning;

3 Abstract Reasoning;

4 Decision Analysis;

5 Non-cognitive Analysis.

There are individual test instructions and separate timed sessions for each sub-test. The total testing time is two hours.

Those candidates with special educational needs sit the UKCATSEN version.

How is it used?

The universities in the UKCAT consortium use the test results in differing ways. Some of the medical and dental schools apply a cut-off – applicants scoring below a certain level will not progress. Other schools do not apply a cut-off score but consider the results alongside other criteria, such as academic performance, a personal statement and an interview. You will need to contact the relevant schools for details of their admissions policies.

What does it test?

This is a test of your numerical reasoning rather than your ability to carry out a maths calculation. Healthcare workers must be able to work accurately with mathematical problems. In the case of a medical professional, quantitative reasoning truly is a matter of life or death. This is not an academic test; it is unlike tests that you took at school. You need to get to know the test format and to start practising. The standard that the test expects is a good Maths GCSE pass.

These practice questions are based on the latest (2008) UKCAT test that was available when the questions were being written. The 2009 format is moving away from presenting all the numerical information in a single chart or graph. However, these practice questions will still give you valuable practice in the mathematical operations that you will need to conduct. The same strategies and test-taking tips apply. The practice questions are based on the mathematical operations that are common to 2008/09. These include the following: money; reading tables, percentages; addition/subtraction; multiplication/division; calculation of mean; and speed/distance/time.

brilliant resources

The Pearson VUE website (http://www.pearsonvue.co.uk) contains a lot of useful information on the UKCAT tests, including a case study and details on how the testing process is managed.

http://www.pearsonvue.co.uk/OurClients/Pages/UKCAT.aspx

The official UKCAT website at http://www.ukcat.ac.uk also provides further introductory information, along with further practice questions and answer explanations.

This website also has an online testing demo to familiarise you with the test format and a Test Centre tour as well as hints and tips.

The Open University website offers free, online maths courses, for example:

http://www.openlearn.open.ac.uk/course/view.php?id=3345

UKCAT – Quantitative Reasoning

Instructions

You will have 1 minute for reading the test instructions, followed by 21 minutes for answering 40 questions. There will be 10 charts, tables or graphs to interpret. Each of these is followed by a set of 4 questions. There are 5 answer options for each of these multiple choice questions. You will be provided with a calculator to use.

The average length of time that you have to answer each question is slightly over 30 seconds. When you practise, try to stick to a 30-second time limit for each question. Of course you will need to allow additional time to read and interpret the information in the initial table or graph.

In addition to getting the calculations right, you need to ensure that the units you use are correct. Always check that you have read the charts and tables accurately.

brilliant tips

● Use a bit of detective work – look for the right information amongst all the figures and statistics provided and then solve the maths problem.

● The graduate-level questions in the next chapter are similar to the UKCAT questions in terms of difficulty level. Have a go at these if you want extra practice. Some are more difficult but well worth practising!

Practice questions

These practice questions have five questions associated with each chart or graph rather than the four you will get in the actual test. The reason is simple: extra questions give you extra practice.

Use the figures provided in the table *Distances (miles and kilometres) of major cities from London* to answer the following five questions.

Distances (miles and kilometres) of major cities from London

Distance from London	Miles	Kilometres
Bombay	4,500	7,000
Chicago	4,000	6,305
Hong Kong	6,025	9,735
Lima	6,315	10,125
Moscow	1,585	2,475
Sydney	10,580	16,970

1   Which of the following statements is true of the cities shown?

(A) Four cities are closer to London than Hong Kong.

(B) Chicago is over 20% closer to London than Bombay.

(C) The range in distances shown in miles is 1,585–10,580.

(D) Bombay is over three times as far away from London as Moscow.

(E) The range in distance (in km) shown is 2,475–10,125.

2   Which two cities are closest to London?

(A) Bombay, Chicago

(B) Chicago, Hong Kong

(C) Hong Kong, Lima

(D) Lima, Moscow

(E) Moscow, Chicago

3   What is the ratio of the distance (in miles) to Bombay compared to Chicago?

(A) 8 : 9

(B) 5 : 4

(C) 9 : 8

(D) 4 : 5

(E) 45 : 40

4   What is the distance in km from Lima to Hong Kong

(A) 4,500

(B) 4,000

(C) 290

(D) 295

(E) Can't say

5   A charter plane flies from London to and from Bombay at an average speed of 700 km per hour. How long will the total flight take?

(A) 20 hours

(B) 19 hours

(C) 18 hours

(D) 17 hours

(E) 16 hours

To answer the following five questions use the figures provided in the pie chart *Percentages of South American electricity produced by five sources: nuclear; gas; coal; oil and renewables.*

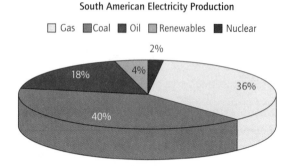

South American Electricity Production

☐ Gas ■ Coal ■ Oil ■ Renewables ■ Nuclear

6   What is the ratio of electricity generated from renewable sources to gas?
(A) 1 : 7
(B) 2 : 7
(C) 1 : 9
(D) 2 : 9
(E) 1 : 11

7   What fraction is oil production of coal production?
(A) $\frac{9}{20}$
(B) $\frac{18}{40}$
(C) $\frac{1}{8}$
(D) $\frac{1}{4}$
(E) $\frac{1}{2}$

8   South American electricity production is 550 GWh. How much is generated by nuclear power?
(A) 5.5 GWh
(B) 4.4 GWh
(C) 3.3 GWh
(D) 2.2 GWh
(E) 1.1 GWh

9   South American electricity production is 700 GWh. What is
     the ratio of electricity generated by coal to gas and renew-
     able sources combined?
     (A) 1 : 1
     (B) 2 : 1
     (C) 1 : 2
     (D) 2 : 3
     (E) 1 : 3

10   South American electricity production is 500 GWh. What
     fraction of the total is generated by coal?
     (A) ⅔
     (B) ½
     (C) ⅖
     (D) ⅔
     (E) ⅕

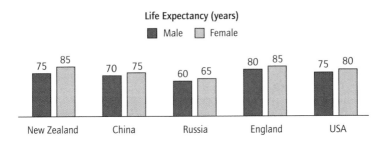

To answer the following five questions refer to the graph *Life
expectancies (in years) for men and women in five countries*.

11   Which of the following statements is false?
     (A) The lowest life expectancy for men is in Russia.
     (B) The range of life expectancy shown for men is 60–80
          years.
     (C) The range of life expectancy shown for women is
          65–85 years.
     (D) The lowest life expectancy for women is in Russia.
     (E) The highest life expectancy for women is in the USA.

12 What is the range of life expectancy for men compared to women?
    (A) Women (65 years); Men (60 years)
    (B) Women (85 years); Men (80 years)
    (C) Men (60-80 years); Women (65-85 years)
    (D) Men (65-85 years); Women (60-85 years)
    (E) Women (60-80 years); Men (65-85 years)

13 What is the average life expectancy for men?
    (A) 71 years
    (B) 71.5 years
    (C) 72 years
    (D) 72.5 years
    (E) 73 years

14 What is the modal life expectancy for women?
    (A) 65 years
    (B) 70 years
    (C) 75 years
    (D) 80 years
    (E) 85 years

15 Which countries have the highest and the lowest overall life expectations?
    (A) Russia, England
    (B) England, Russia
    (C) England, USA
    (D) USA, China
    (E) England, China

Use the figures provided in the table *Time zones for several cities around the world at 12.00 hrs in London* to answer the following five questions.

Time zones for several cities around the world at 12.00 hrs in London

City	Local time
Berlin	13.00 hrs
Cairo	14.00 hrs
Chicago	06.00 hrs
Delhi	17.30 hrs
Edinburgh	12.00 hrs
Karachi	17.00 hrs
Melbourne	22.00 hrs
New York	07.00 hrs
Reykjavik	11.00 hrs
Singapore	19.30 hrs

16   What is the time difference in New York compared to Delhi?

(A) 10 hours 30 mins ahead

(B) 10 hours 30 mins behind

(C) 11 hours 30 mins ahead

(D) 11 hours 30 mins behind

(E) 12 hours 30 mins behind

17   What is the time in Singapore when it is 09.00 in London?

(A) 16.30 hrs

(B) 17.30 hrs

(C) 18.30 hrs

(D) 19.30 hrs

(E) 20.30 hrs

18   A plane leaves London 19.30 local time and arrives in New York at 21.00 local time. How long was the flight?

(A) 5.5 hours

(B) 6 hours

(C) 6.5 hours

(D) 7 hours

(E) 7.5 hours

19 What time is it in Reyjavik if it is 16.30 hrs in London?

   (A) 13.30 hrs

   (B) 14.00 hrs

   (C) 14.30 hrs

   (D) 15.00 hrs

   (E) 15.30 hrs

20 A plane leaves London at 20.00 hrs traveling at 500 mph. The distance to Chicago is 4,000 miles. What local time does it arrive?

   (A) 21.00 hrs

   (B) 21.30 hrs

   (C) 22.00 hrs

   (D) 22.30 hrs

   (E) 23.00 hrs

Use the figures provided in the graph *Monthly rental income for two properties (Houses A and B) for 2003–2008* to answer the following five questions.

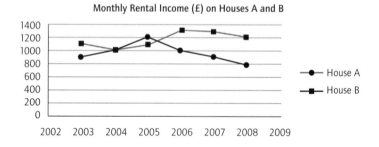

21 What is the change in House B's monthly rental income between 2003 and 2004?

   (A) £100 increase

   (B) £100 decrease

   (C) £150 increase

   (D) £150 decrease

   (E) £200 increase

22 What is the overall change in House A's monthly rental income between 2004 and 2006?

(A) £300 decrease

(B) £200 decrease

(C) £0

(D) £200 increase

(E) £300 increase

23 What is the difference in House B's income for 2007 compared to 2003?

(A) £0

(B) £1,200

(C) £2,400

(D) £4,800

(E) £7,200

24 What is the difference in House A's monthly rental income for 2003 compared to 2008?

(A) £100 less (per month)

(B) £100 more (per month)

(C) £200 less (per month)

(D) £200 more (per month)

(E) No difference

25 Between which years is there the same difference in rental income across Houses A and B?

(A) 2003, 2006

(B) 2005, 2006

(C) 2006, 2007

(D) 2007, 2008

(E) 2006, 2007

Use the figures provided in the table *Approximate sizes (in square miles) of several key islands, oceans and seas* to answer the following five questions.

Approximate sizes (in square miles) of several key islands, oceans and seas

Island	Square miles
Borneo	287,050
Greenland	839,700
Honshu	88,950
Victoria	82,300

Body of water	Square miles
Atlantic Ocean	31,799,900
Caribbean Sea	1,063,075
Gulf of Mexico	596,050
South China Sea	1,148,850

26   Which of the following statements is true?
   (A) Lake Honshu is less than 5% larger than Lake Victoria.
   (B) The largest island is smaller than the smallest body of water.
   (C) The largest body of water is bigger than the combined area of all four islands.
   (D) The Caribbean Sea is the second biggest body of water shown.
   (E) Greenland is less than twice the size of the other islands shown.

27   Which are the smallest and the largest of all islands and bodies of water shown?
   (A) Borneo, Atlantic Ocean
   (B) Victoria, South China Sea
   (C) Honshu, South China Sea
   (D) Honshu, Atlantic Ocean
   (E) Victoria, Atlantic Ocean

28   What is the total size of the islands shown (in square miles)?
   (A) 1,198,000
   (B) 1,298,000
   (C) 1,398,000
   (D) 1,498,000
   (E) 1,598,000

29   What percentage of the total area of water shown is the Atlantic Ocean (to the nearest whole number)?

(A) 90%

(B) 91%

(C) 92%

(D) 93%

(E) 95%

30   What is the difference in size (in square miles) between the smallest and the largest bodies of water?

(A) 31,203,950

(B) 31,203,900

(C) 31,203,850

(D) 31,203,800

(E) 31,203,750

To answer the following five questions refer to the table *Cost of monthly and annual subscriptions for magazines a to e.*

Cost of monthly and annual subscriptions for magazines a to e

	Magazines a–e				
	a	b	c	d	e
Annual fee (£)	49.00	59.00	54.99	55.99	49.99
Monthly fee (£)	5.00	6.00	5.49	5.99	4.99

31   What is the cost of taking out monthly subscriptions for 18 months with magazines a, b and d?

(A) £74.99

(B) £88.50

(C) £265.93

(D) £305.82

(E) £323.64

32 What is the total cost of 6 months' subscription to all mag-
    azines?
    (A) £161.82
    (B) £164.82
    (C) £167.82
    (D) £170.82
    (E) £173.82

33 Which magazine offers the greatest saving in taking out an
    annual subscription rather than a monthly subscription?
    (A) Magazine a
    (B) Magazine b
    (C) Magazine c
    (D) Magazine d
    (E) Magazine e

34 Which magazine offers the least saving in taking out an
    annual subscription rather than a monthly subscription?
    (A) Magazine a
    (B) Magazine b
    (C) Magazine c
    (D) Magazine d
    (E) Magazine e

35 The cost of monthly contract 'a' rises by 15%. What is the
    new cost of 6 monthly payments?
    (A) £30.00
    (B) £32.50
    (C) £34.50
    (D) £35.00
    (E) £36.50

To answer the following five questions refer to the pie charts
showing the *Percentages of different sources of Australian electricity
demand (actual 2008 and projected figures for 2050)*.

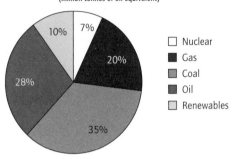

2008 Australian Electricity Demand
(million tonnes of oil equivalent)

□ Nuclear
■ Gas
■ Coal
■ Oil
□ Renewables

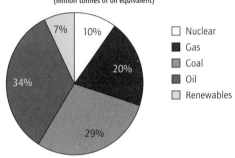

2050 Australian Electricity Demand
(million tonnes of oil equivalent)

□ Nuclear
■ Gas
■ Coal
■ Oil
□ Renewables

36 What is the 2008 demand ratio between gas, renewables and coal?
    (A) $2:1:3$
    (B) $3:2:5$
    (C) $3:2:7$
    (D) $4:2:5$
    (E) $4:2:7$

37 What fraction of total electricity production for 2008 are gas and coal respectively?
    (A) $\frac{1}{5}$; $\frac{7}{20}$
    (B) $\frac{7}{20}$; $\frac{1}{5}$
    (C) $\frac{1}{3}$; $\frac{7}{20}$
    (D) $\frac{7}{10}$; $\frac{1}{3}$
    (E) $\frac{1}{3}$; $\frac{7}{10}$

38   The total Australian electricity demand is 280 billion kWh
     in 2008. How much of this is produced by gas?
     (A) 28 billion kWh
     (B) 42 billion kWh
     (C) 56 billion kWh
     (D) 70 billion kWh
     (E) 84 billion kWh

39   Between 2008 and 2050 the production of Australian elec-
     tricity demand from renewables is forecast to change by
     what percentage?
     (A) 3% more
     (B) 3% less
     (C) 13% more
     (D) 13% less
     (E) 10% less

40   Between 2008 and 2050 which form of electricity gener-
     ation exhibits the least change?
     (A) Gas
     (B) Nuclear
     (C) Coal
     (D) Oil
     (E) Renewables

Use the figures provided in the *Timetables of weekday and Sunday
train times from Keen* to answer the following five questions.

Timetables of weekday and Sunday train times from Keen

| Mondays to Saturdays | | | | | |
DESTINATION	TRAIN TIMES				
Keen train station	0630	0730	0830	Then at	1445	1545
Brume	0646	0746	0846	these mins	1501	1601
Gingford	0657	0757	0857	past each	1512	1612
Kisley	0715	0815	0915	hour until	1530	1630
Detton Central	0728	0828	0928		1543	1643

Sundays DESTINATION	TRAIN TIMES			
Keen train station	0730	0845	then at	2045
Brume	0747	0902	these mins	2102
Gingford	0758	0913	past each	2113
Kisley	0816	0931	hour until	2131
Detton Central	0829	0944		2144
	There is no Bank Holiday service on this line			

41 How long does a train journey take between Brume and Kisley on a Wednesday?

(A) 21 mins

(B) 23 mins

(C) 25 mins

(D) 27 mins

(E) 29 mins

42 What is the time difference between the Sunday and the weekly train service?

(A) 2 minutes slower

(B) 1 minute slower

(C) No time difference

(D) 1 minute faster

(E) 2 minutes faster

43 Due to engineering works the Sunday train service is replaced by a bus between Detton Central and Gingford. The bus takes 20 mins longer than the train service. What time can a passenger taking the 08.45 hrs train from Keen expect to arrive in Detton Central?

(A) 09.13 hrs

(B) 09.44 hrs

(C) 09.54 hrs

(D) 10.04 hrs

(E) 10.14 hrs

44   What time does the 13.46 hrs Monday train leaving Brume
     arrive in Detton Central?
     (A) 14.28 hrs
     (B) 14.29 hrs
     (C) 14.30 hrs
     (D) 14.31 hrs
     (E) 14.32 hrs

45   At what average speed does the weekday train travel the 18
     miles between Gingford and Kisley?
     (A) 18 mph
     (B) 28 mph
     (C) 40 mph
     (D) 50 mph
     (E) 60 mph

Use the figures provided in the table *Simple interest paid on £10
at different interest rates* to answer the following five questions.

Simple interest added to £10 at different interest rates

Time frame	Interest rate			
	7%	8%	9%	15%
1 year	10.7	10.8	10.9	11.5
5 years	13.5	14	14.5	17.5
10 years	17	18	19	25
50 years	45	50	55	85

46   What is the interest paid on £15 over 10 years at 9%?
     (A) £13.50
     (B) £14.50
     (C) £18.00
     (D) £19.00
     (E) £28.50

47 What is the value of £200 invested in a 7% account at the end of 5 years?
(A) £230
(B) £240
(C) £250
(D) £260
(E) £270

48 What is the difference in value between Account A (paying 8% interest) and Account B (paying 7% interest) on £10 over 50 years?
(A) £4.00
(B) £4.50
(C) £5.00
(D) £45.00
(E) £50.00

49 What is the difference in interest paid on £25 over 5 years at 7% and 15%?
(A) £10.00
(B) £13.50
(C) £17.50
(D) £25.00
(E) £33.75

50 The interest rate payable changes from 7% in the first year to 8% in the second year. How much interest does £50 earn over this two-year period?
(A) £3.50
(B) £4.28
(C) £7.50
(D) £7.78
(E) £10.70

Quantitative Reasoning answers

Question	Answer
1	(C)
2	(E) Moscow, Chicago
3	(C) 9 : 8
4	(E) Can't say
5	(A) 20 hours
6	(C) 1 : 9
7	(A) $\frac{9}{20}$
8	(E) 1.1 GWh
9	(A) 1 : 1
10	(C) $\frac{2}{5}$
11	(E) The highest life expectancy for women is in the USA.
12	(C) Men (60–80 years); Women (65–85 years)
13	(C) 72 years
14	(E) 85 years
15	(B) England, Russia
16	(B) 10 hours 30 mins behind
17	(A) 16.30 hrs
18	(C) 6.5 hours
19	(E) 15.30 hrs
20	(C) 22.00 hrs
21	(B) £100 decrease
22	(E) £300 increase
23	(C) £2,400
24	(A) £100 less (per month)
25	(D) 2007, 2008
26	(C) The largest body of water is bigger than the combined area of all four islands.
27	(E) Victoria, Atlantic Ocean
28	(B) 1,298,000
29	(C) 92%
30	(E) 31,203,850

31	(D) £305.82
32	(B) £164.82
33	(D) Magazine d
34	(E) Magazine e
35	(C) £34.50
36	(E) 4 : 2 : 7
37	(A) ⅕; ⁷⁄₂₀
38	(C) 56 billion kWh
39	(B) 3% less
40	(A) Gas
41	(E) 29 mins
42	(B) 1 minute slower
43	(D) 10.04 hrs
44	(A) 14.28 hrs
45	(E) 60 mph
46	(A) £13.50
47	(E) £270
48	(C) £5.00
49	(A) £10.00
50	(D) £7.78

Additional answer explanations

1   (C)
The range in distances shown in miles is 1,585–10,580

> **brilliant tip**
>
> Once you have found a True statement then move on to the next question.

2   (E) Moscow, Chicago
Step 1 – Find two lowest distances
Moscow = 1,585 miles
Chicago = 4,000 miles

3   (C) 9 : 8

Step 1 – Form a ratio of the two distances

4500 : 4000

Step 2 – Find the highest common denominator

This is the number that both numbers can be divided by and still leave two whole numbers

The highest common denominator = 500

Step 3 – Simplify the ratio by dividing by the highest common denominator

4500/500 : 4000/500 is the same as 9 : 8

brilliant tip

Note that answer option E (45 : 40) is the same ratio as the correct answer. However one more stage is needed; to simplify the ratio by dividing both numbers by the highest common denominator.

4   (E) Can't say

The distances are only given from London. You could calculate the difference in the distances from London. However, this is not the same as the difference in distance between the two cities.

5   (A) 20 hours

Step 1 – Calculate the total distance in km

7,000 × 2 = 14,000 km

Step 2 – Calculate the total flight time

14,000/700 = 20 hours

brilliant warning

Read the question carefully: flies to and from Hong Kong.

6 (C) 1 : 9

Step 1 – Put the two percentages into a ratio

4 : 36

Step 2 – Calculate the highest common denominator

Highest common denominator = largest number that both 4 and 36 are divisible by

Step 3 – Divide by the highest common denominator

4/4 : 36/4 = 1:9

7 (A) 9/20

Step 1 – Change the percentages to a fraction

18% : 40%

Step 2 – Calculate the highest common denominator

Highest common denominator = 2

18/2 = 9

40/2 = 20

Fraction = 9/20

8 (E) 1.1 GWh

Step 1 – Calculate % figure

55 GWh × 2%/100 = 1.1 GWh

9 (A) 1 : 1

Do not be distracted by the production figure provided. The calculation does not require you to use this figure.

Step 1 – Calculate the total % for gas and renewable sources

36% + 4% = 40%

Step 2 – Calculate the ratio

40% : 40% = 1 : 1

10 (C) 2/5

Step 1 – Convert % into a fraction

40% = 2/5

There is no need to calculate the figure in GWh for electricity generated by coal.

11 (E) The highest life expectancy for women is in the USA.
Step 1 – Check statement against graph
The life expectancy for women in the USA is 80 years.
The highest life expectancy shown is 85 years, so the statement is false.

12 (C) Men (60–80 years); Women (65–85 years)

13 (C) 72 years
Step 1 – Calculate the average
(60 + 70 + 75 + 75 + 80) / 5 = 360 / 5 = 72

14 (E) 85 years
Step 1 – Select the most popular life expectancy for women
There are two countries where the life expectancy for women is 85 years (and) so this is the most popular, given that all the other life expectancies only occur once.
The definition of the modal or modal score is the most popular, i.e. the score with the highest frequency of occurrences.

15 (B) England, Russia

16 (B) 10 hours 30 mins behind
Step 1 – Calculate the time difference between New York and Delhi
Both times are relative to London so the difference between the two cities is the difference between the two cities (when it is the same 12.00 hrs in London)
17.30 hrs − 07.00 hrs = 10 hours 30 mins
Step 2 – New York time is shown as behind, i.e. earlier than Delhi
So the correct answer is 10 hours 30 mins behind

17 (A) 16.30 hrs
Step 1 – Calculate the time difference between Singapore and London
19.30 hrs − 12.00 hrs = 7 hours 30 minutes

So Singapore is seven and a half hours ahead of London.
Step 2 – Apply this time difference to nine o'clock in the morning in London (09.00 hrs)
If it is 09.00 hrs in London then in Singapore it is 09.00 hrs + 7.5 hours ahead
So in 24-hour clock terms, the time in Singapore is 16.30 hrs

18   (C) 6.5 hours
Step 1 – Calculate the time difference between the two cities
07.00 hrs (New York); 12.00 hrs (London) means that New York is 5 hours behind London
Step 2 – Use New York time to calculate the flight time
Basing the answer on New York local time; the plane leaves London at 14.30 hrs (19.30 hrs − 5 hours) then takes 21.00 hrs − 14.30 hrs = 6.5 hours to arrive in New York at 21.00 hrs local time.

19   (E) 15.30 hrs
Step 1 – Calculate the time difference
Reyjavik is 12.00 hrs − 11.00 hrs = 1 hour behind
Step 2 – Apply the time difference
16.30 hrs − 1 hour = 15.30 hrs

20   (C) 22.00 hrs
Step 1 – Calculate the flight time
4000 / 500 = 8 hour flight
Step 2 – Calculate the time difference between London and Chicago
12.00 hrs (London); 06.00 hrs (Chicago) means that Chicago is 6 hours behind London
Local time refers to the time in Chicago rather than London time.
Step 3 – Calculate local time when plane leaves

London time (20.00 hrs) is 20.00 hrs − 6 hours = 14.00 hrs in Chicago.
Step 4 – Calculate local time of arrival
Add 8 hour flight time to 14.00 hrs = 22.00 hrs

21 (B) £100 decrease

22 (E) £300 increase
£1,300 (in 2006) − £1,000 (in 2004) = £300 increase

23 (C) £2,400
Step 1 – Calculate the total difference in rental income for each year
2003: 1,100 × 12 = £13,200
2007: 1,300 × 12 = £15,600
£15,600 − £13,200 = £2,400

24 (A) £100 less (per month)
Step 1 – Calculate the difference between the 2 graph readings
2008 = £1,200 per month
2003 = £1,100 per month
Difference = £1,200 − £1,100 = £100 less (per month)

25 (D) 2007, 2008

26 (C) The largest body of water is bigger than the combined area of all four islands.
Step 1 – Calculate the combined area of all four islands
287,050 + 839,700 + 88,950 + 82,300 = 1,298,000 square miles
Step 2 – Compare to see which is bigger
Largest body of water (Atlantic Ocean) = 31,799,900 which is bigger than the combined area of all four islands.

27 (E) Victoria, Atlantic Ocean
Step 1 – Calculate total area of water
31,799,900 + 1,063,075 + 596,050 + 1,148,850 = 34,607,875

Step 2 – Calculate %

100 × 31,799,900 / 34,607,875 = 91.8%

Step 3 – To the nearest whole number

.8 is greater than .5 and therefore 91.8% needs to be rounded up to 92%

28 (B) 1,298,000

Total size = 287,050 + 839,700 + 88,950 + 82,300 = 1,298,000 square miles

29 (C) 92%

Step 1 – Total area = 31,799,900 + 1,063,075 + 596,050 + 1,148,850 = 34,607,875

Step 2 – Atlantic Ocean = 100 × 31,799,900/34,607,875 = 91.89%

Step 3 – to nearest whole number = 92%

30 (E) 31,203,850

31,799,900 (Atlantic Ocean) − 596,050 (Gulf of Mexico) = 31,203,850

31 (D) £305.82

Step 1 – Calculate the total monthly cost for all three magazines

5.00 + 6.00 + 5.99 = 16.99

Step 2 – Calculate the cost for 18 months

16.99 × 18 = £305.82

Note that the question stresses monthly subscriptions. The answer option £265.93 is the correct answer if the calculation was 6 monthly subscriptions, together with an annual subscription (for the other 12 months).

tips

- This question can be answered in two steps only – rather than doing three separate calculations for the three magazines. Make the addition calculation first (5.00 + 6.00 + 5.99). Then the total cost for 18 months.

- Another short-cut is to calculate 17 × 18 and then to deduct the 18p from your total.

32 (B) £164.82

$6 \times (£5 + £6 + £5.49 + £5.99 + £4.99) = £164.82$

33 (D) Magazine d

Step 1 – Calculate each subscription's total monthly cost for a year's worth of monthly payments

Magazine a = $12 \times £5 = £60$

Magazine b = $12 \times £6 = £72$

Magazine c = $12 \times £5.49 = £65.88$

Magazine d = $12 \times £5.99 = £71.88$

Magazine e = $12 \times £4.99 = £59.88$

Step 2 – Calculate the difference for each subscription with the annual fee

Magazine a = $£60 – £49 = £11.00$

Magazine b = $£72 – £59 = £13.00$

Magazine c = $£65.88 – £54.99 = £13.00$

Magazine d = $£71.88 – £55.99 = £15.89$

Magazine e = $£59.88 – £49.99 = £9.89$

34 (E) Magazine e

35 (C) £34.50

Step 1 – Calculate the new monthly fee

$£5.00 \times 115\% / 100 = £5.75$

Step 2 – Calculate the cost for 6 months

$£5.75 \times 6 = £34.50$

36 (E) 4 : 2 : 7
Step 1 – Put percent into a ratio
20 : 10 : 35
Step 2 – Simplify ratio
4 : 2 : 7

37 (A) $\frac{1}{5}$; $\frac{7}{20}$
Step 1 – Convert each percentage to a fraction
Gas; 20% = $\frac{20}{100}$
Coal; 35% = $\frac{35}{100}$
Step 2 – Simplify fractions by dividing by highest common denominator
Gas (highest common denominator = 20)
$\frac{20}{120}$ = (20/20) / (120/20) = $\frac{1}{5}$
Coal (highest common denominator = 5)
$\frac{35}{100}$ = (35/5) / (100/5) = $\frac{7}{20}$

38 (C) 56 billion kWh
Step 1 – Read % from 2008 pie chart
Gas = 20%
Step 2 – Calculate % amount using the total production figure supplied
280 × 20 / 100 = 56 billion kWh

39 (B) 3% less
The change from 7% to 10% represents 3% less

40 (A) Gas

41 (E) 29 mins
Step 1 – Read one of the sets of timetable – times between the two locations
Brume (06.47 hrs) to Kisley (07.16 hrs)
Step 2 – Calculate the time difference
07.16 hrs − 06.47 hrs = 29 mins difference

42 (B) 1 minute slower

43 (D) 10.04 hrs
Step 1 – Read the timetabled time that the 08.45 hrs train service normally arrives
Step 2 – Add 20 mins to this time
09.44 hrs + 20 mins = 10.04 hrs

44 (A) 14.28 hrs

45 (E) 60 mph
Step 1 – Calculate the journey time from the timetable
07.16 hrs − 06.58 hrs = 18 mins = 18/60 hours
Step 2 – Calculate average speed
Average speed = distance / time = 18 miles / (18 / 60 hours) = 60 mph

46 (A) £13.50
Step 1 – Read from the table the 9% rate
Interest paid over 10 years at a 9% rate = £19 (for a £10 principal sum deposited)
Step 2 – Calculate how much £15 would increase
£19 × £15 / £10 = £28.50
Step 3 – Calculate how much of this is interest
£28.50 − £15.00 = £13.50

47 (E) £270
Step 1 – Read from the table the appropriate investment amount
£13.50
Step 2 – Calculate the investment amount for £200
£13.50 × £200 / £10 = £270

48 (C) £5.00
Step 1 – Read from the table the appropriate investment amounts
£45.00 (7%) and £50.00 (8%)
Step 2 – Calculate the difference
£50.00 − £45.00 = £5.00

49 (A) £10.00

Step 1 – Read from the table the 7% and 15% rates

Interest paid over 5 years at 7% and 15% rates = £13.50 and £17.50 (for a £10 principal sum deposited)

Step 2 – Calculate how much £25 increases to at the 7% and 15% rates

£13.50 × £25/£10 = £33.75

£17.50 × £25/£10 = £43.75

Step 3 – Calculate the difference

£43.75 − £33.75 = £10.00

50 (D) £7.78

Step 1 – Read from the table the 7% for £10 = £10.70 (at 7%)

Step 2 – Calculate the increased value of £50 by the end of the first year

£10.70 × £50 / £10 = £53.50 (interest = £3.50)

Step 3 – Calculate the interest for £53.50 in the second year at 8%

£53.50 × 8% / 100 = £4.28

Step 3 – Add the two interest amounts

£3.50 + £4.28 = £7.78

brilliant tips

- There are many calculations involved in this question. This is the sort of question that for time efficiency reasons you need to leave until last.

- Simple interest involves a percentage calculation. As has been done in this question it is possible to work out such percentage increases without reference to the table.

CHAPTER 9

Graduate-level numeracy tests

I n today's fiercely competitive business world, organisations only want to invest in the most promising graduate trainees. As the number of graduates has increased dramatically in recent years, employers have turned to ability tests in order to distinguish between many qualified applicants. Numeracy tests are one effective way of assessing large numbers of graduates. As a result, they are commonly used on the graduate milk round. You are also likely to encounter them at an interview for a first or second job. You could also be asked to take a graduate-level numeracy test as part of a development programme, or if you are receiving career guidance to see how you would fare when dealing with lots of complex numerical information.

How are they taken?

These tests are available in both pencil-and-paper and online formats. Typically, if you pass an online numeracy test you will be given a follow-up test at a later date. As a rule of thumb, the tests usually contain between 20 and 40 questions and have a time limit ranging from 25 to 35 minutes. You will be able to use a calculator to answer the questions.

What do they look like?

Expect to be given a set of figures in either a table or a graph, followed by several questions that ask you to interpret and manipulate these figures. You might be given line graphs, bar charts, pie charts – any format that can appear in business and professional reports. There may be text-based questions, graph-based questions or a combination of both, as per the practice questions here.

It is worth thinking about the types of tables and graphs that you would encounter in a business context: sales figures, attendance figures, costs, budgets, and such like. That's exactly the sort of thing that appears in these tests.

How hard are they?

Just as there is a range of numerical ability amongst the graduate population, graduate numeracy tests also vary in difficulty level. The difficulty of the test you encounter will reflect the degree of numerical complexity involved in the role you are applying for. If the job is in Accounts or involves managing large projects then you should expect to be given one of the more difficult numeracy tests. Graduate numeracy test questions will invariably be set in a work context and will require you to interpret complex numerical information.

If you want additional practice, you can answer the questions in Chapters 8 and 10. The hardest UKCAT questions are of a comparable standard to graduate-level tests. The senior managerial questions are more difficult than graduate-level tests, and thus are a great way to challenge yourself in your practice sessions.

↗ brilliant resources

There are many websites that offer free practice opportunities for this popular test format. Search under 'numerical reasoning test practice' and take your pick of the sites.

Instructions

Always read every single word in the question very carefully. Think through what the question is asking before diving into the calculation.

Remember that the average length of time that you should use to answer each question is approximately one minute. Try to stick to this time limit when you complete the practice questions.

✦ brilliant tips

- Keep things simple whenever possible so that you can focus on getting the calculation correct.

- Don't be distracted by complex business language, the size of the figures or the measurement units. Nine times out of ten the measurement units will be constant throughout the question and answer.

- Also, if you can get the right answer by doing a rough calculation then by all means do so.

- Similarly, if you can get to the answer by looking at trends in the graph then great! Rather than spending valuable time on a calculation you may only need to scan the graph to see where, for example, the biggest and smallest differences occur.

Practice questions

1   A financial company's balance sheet includes property assets of £212 million and £40 million in derivative assets. What is the effect on the balance sheet of the property assets rising by a quarter and the derivative assets dropping by three tenths?

(A) £265 million lower

(B) £41 million lower

    (C) £12 million lower

    (D) £41 million higher

    (E) £265 million higher

2   The sales of a multinational company are $480,000 in the Asia-Pacific region and $440,000 in the European region. If the total worldwide sales are $1,150,000, what fraction do these two regions represent?

    (A) ⅕

    (B) ⅖

    (C) ⅗

    (D) ⅔

    (E) ⅘

3   The total assets of an oil company are $950 million in North America and $178 million in Canada. What percentage are these of the total company assets of $9,400 million?

    (A) 9.4%

    (B) 10%

    (C) 10.4%

    (D) 12%

    (E) 12.4%

4   A transatlantic company's quarterly costs are $48,000 in their sales division and $64,000 in their marketing division. What is the ratio of the sales to marketing costs?

    (A) 2 : 3

    (B) 3 : 2

    (C) 3 : 4

    (D) 4 : 3

    (E) 3 : 5

5   The global marketplace for outsourcing has been predicted to grow from £234,000 million in 2008 to £319,000 million in 2011. What is the total percentage increase predicted to be over these three years (to one decimal place)?

(A) None of these
(B) 12.1%
(C) 24.2%
(D) 36.3%
(E) 48.4%

6   In an employee survey of 225 employees the response rate was 6 out of 10. How many employees did not complete the survey?
(A) 40
(B) 60
(C) 90
(D) 135
(E) Can't tell

Use the figures provided in the table *Pension fund shareholdings of Company Inc. shares* to answer the following three questions.

Pension fund shareholdings of Company Inc. shares (priced at £3.25)

	Number of shares
Pension fund A	40,500
Pension fund B	36,750
Pension fund C	25,400
Pension fund D	22,300
Pension fund E	18,250

7   Which pension fund has shares worth £82,550?
(A) Pension fund A
(B) Pension fund B
(C) Pension fund C
(D) Pension fund D
(E) Pension fund E

8   If pension fund A's shareholding represents 20.25% of all Company Inc. shares, how many Company Inc. shares are there in total?
(A) 19,000

(B) 20,000
(C) 25,000
(D) 200,000
(E) 250,000

9   What is the average value of the five pension funds (to the nearest £1,000)?
(A) £93,000
(B) £93,100
(C) £95,000
(D) £97,000
(E) £99,000

10   On a salary survey 9 out of every 20 staff were in the £20,000 to £30,000 pay band. If the total salary pay roll is £460,000 per month, what is the average employee salary?
(A) Can't tell
(B) £15,000
(C) £20,000
(D) £25,000
(E) £30,000

11   A Finance Director who earns a salary of £360,000 also receives 0.35 of this salary as an annual bonus payment. What is the Finance Director's total salary and bonus package worth?
(A) £450,000
(B) £468,000
(C) £486,000
(D) £504,000
(E) £522,000

12   Washing machine brand A sells three times as many units per month as washing machine brand B. If the total monthly sales of the two washing machines is £440,000, what value of washing machine B are sold on average per month?

(A) £100,000
(B) £110,000
(C) £111,000
(D) £125,000
(E) £150,000

Use the figures provided in the graph *Coal demand (million tonnes) for imported and indigenous supplies for Years 1 to 5* to answer questions 13–16.

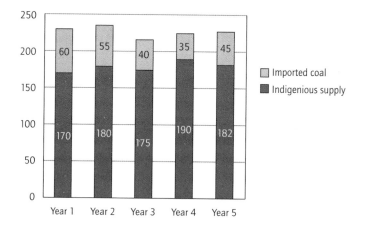

13 What has been the average amount of imported coal over the five years shown?
(A) 40 million tonnes
(B) 44 million tonnes
(C) 47 million tonnes
(D) 50 million tonnes
(E) 54 million tonnes

14 In which year was the coal demand met from imported coal the lowest relative to that met from indigenous sources?
(A) Year 1
(B) Year 2
(C) Year 3
(D) Year 4
(E) Year 5

15   The total coal demand for each year is the sum of the imported and indigeneous supply figures. Put the total coal demand for each year in size order, starting with the highest.

(A)   Year 2, Year 1, Year 5, Year 4, Year 3

(B)   Year 2, Year 1, Year 4, Year 5, Year 3

(C)   Year 2, Year 1, Year 4, Year 3, Year 5

(D)   Year 2, Year 5, Year 1, Year 4, Year 3

(E)   Year 2, Year 5, Year 1, Year 3, Year 4

16   Between which years was there the greatest proportional change in the coal demand from indigenous supplies?

(A)   Years 1–2

(B)   Years 2–3

(C)   Years 3–4

(D)   Years 4–5

(E)   Can't tell

17   A company's value increased by 4% in Year 1, 5% in Year 2 and 4.5% in Year 3. If the company was valued at £2.15 million at the start of Year 1 then what is its value at the end of Year 3?

(A)   £2.41 million

(B)   £2.44 million

(C)   £2.45 million

(D)   £24.1 million

(E)   £24.5 million

18   The total cost for a litre of milk is 24.5p. What is the profit (to the nearest £) on 2,500 gallons of milk that is sold in 2-litre cartons for £1.05 (1 gallon = 4.546 litres)?

(A)   £5,967

(B)   £3,182

(C)   £2,784

(D)   £597

(E)   £318

19   A sales rep is deciding whether to fill his 11-gallon petrol
     tank with unleaded (85.2p per litre) or super unleaded
     petrol (91.5p per litre). What is the cost difference (at 4.5
     litres to a gallon)?
     (A) £3.12
     (B) £4.43
     (C) £4.44
     (D) £4.45
     (E) £31.20

20   A retail company's monthly export of clothes rises by a
     quarter from £96,000. How much is the new monthly
     export of clothes?
     (A) £80,000
     (B) £90,000
     (C) £100,000
     (D) £110,000
     (E) £120,000

21   The average manufacturing costs for car manufacturers A
     and B are $950 and $1,390 per car respectively. What is the
     difference in total manufacturing costs if each car manufac-
     turer makes 500 cars?
     (A) $220,000
     (B) $210,000
     (C) $180,000
     (D) $175,000
     (A) $30,000

Use the figures provided in the table *Teams A to E Current budget
($) and cuts for next year* to answer questions 22–24.

Teams A to E current budget ($) and cuts for next year

	Current budget ($)	Cut for next year
Team A	900	5%
Team B	1,350	12%
Team C	400	7.5%
Team D	750	8%
Team E	1,500	12.5%

22   At an exchange rate of $1.46 to the £, what is the total budget cut for next year (to the nearest £)?
   (A) £320
   (B) £332
   (C) £342
   (D) £350
   (E) £375

23   For which team(s) will next year's budget be cut by over $200?
   (A) Team B & C
   (B) Team B & E
   (C) Team B
   (D) Team C
   (E) None of these

24   What is the overall % cut in next year's budget (for all five teams)?
   (A) 9.9%
   (B) 9.6%
   (C) 4.7%
   (D) 1.9%
   (E) 0.8%

25   There is a 0.125 wastage cost when manufacturing steel. What is this as a fraction of overall cost?
   (A) ⅛
   (B) ⅐

(C) ⅙

(D) ⅕

(E) ¼

26   The £5,500 total weekly sales of mobile phones in a retail store increased during a sale by one twentieth for two weeks during a four-week month. What are the total monthly sales (assuming weekly sales remained unchanged in the other two weeks)?

(A) £11,550

(B) £14,550

(C) £17,550

(D) £19,550

(E) £22,550

To answer questions 27–30 use the table *Region a to e's sales (£100,000s) for 2006–2008.*

Region a to e's sales (£100,000s) for 2006–2008

	2006 sales (£100,000s)	2007 sales (£100,000s)	2008 sales (£100,000s)
Region a	1.82	1.64	1.29
Region b	0.45	0.52	0.31
Region c	5.37	6.11	5.91
Region d	5.20	5.86	5.88
Region e	2.34	2.79	2.05

27   In which three regions did sales decrease between 2006 and 2008?

(A) a, b, c

(B) a, b, d

(C) a, b, e

(D) b, c, d

(E) b, c, e

28   In which region was there the greatest proportionate change in sales value between 2007 and 2008?

(A) Region a

(B)   Region b
(C)   Region c
(D)   Region d
(E)   Region e

29   Which region was the highest performer in 2006, 2007 and 2008?
(A)   Region a
(B)   Region b
(C)   Region c
(D)   Region d
(E)   Region e

30   A company pays an interim dividend of 6.2 pence per company share. A shareholder has 3,250 shares. What is the total value of their interim dividend payment?
(A)   £201.50
(B)   £211.50
(C)   £325.00
(D)   £2,015.00
(E)   £3,250.00

Use the figures provided in the graph *Office paper supply and demand (tonnes) for Months 1 to 5* to answer questions 31–34.

Office paper supply and demand (tonnes)

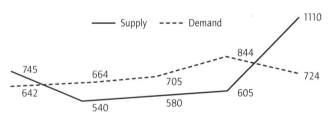

Month 1	Month 2	Month 3	Month 4	Month 5

31 In which month(s) was the office paper demand the most in excess of the office paper supply?

(A) Month 1

(B) Months 1 and 2

(C) Months 2 and 3

(D) Month 4

(E) Month 5

32 Over the five-month period what is the total difference between supply and demand?

(A) 1 tonne

(B) 2 tonnes

(C) 3 tonnes

(D) 4 tonnes

(E) 5 tonnes

33 In which month was there a 103 tonnes difference in supply and demand?

(A) Month 1

(B) Month 2

(C) Month 3

(D) Month 4

(E) Month 5

34 For how many months does supply exceed demand?

(A) 1 month

(B) 2 months

(C) 3 months

(D) 4 months

(E) 5 months

35 An Internet company pays corporation tax at 21%. If the amount of corporation tax paid is £143,850, how much are the company's taxable profits (in £1,000s)?

(A) 80

(B) 600

(C) 650

(D) 680

(E) 685

36 Market expectations are that a house builder's annual profits will fall by 35%. If the previous year's annual profits were £4.6 million what are the expected profits for the current year (in £100,000s)?

(A) 29.70

(B) 29.90

(C) 30.10

(D) 2.97

(E) 2.99

Use the figures provided in the table *Passenger numbers (10,000s) for airlines A and B January to June* to answer question 37.

Passenger numbers (10,000s) for airlines A and B January to June

Passengers (10,000s)	Airline A	Airline B
January	48.1	45.3
February	40.2	48.3
March	42.3	45.8
April	47	45.4
May	45.2	49
June	45.6	48.2

37 In which month was there the second greatest difference in passenger numbers between the two airlines?

(A) January

(B) February

(C) March

(D) April

(E) May

38 In France the monthly sales of a new cosmetics product were €60,600. If the sales in Germany and Spain were each a third of this, what was the total sales across the three European countries (in Euros)?

(A) €101,000

(B) €100,000

(C) €91,000

(D) €11,000

(E) €10,100

39   A multinational shipping company has annual profits of $42.6 million. What is this in £ (at an exchange rate of $1.4 to the £)?

(A) £300 million

(B) £30.61 million

(C) £30.52 million

(D) £30.43 million

(E) £30 million

40   At an exchange rate of 1.2 Euros to the £, what is the cost (in £) of three boxes of office paper at €6.6 per box?

(A) £12.50

(B) £14.50

(C) £16.50

(D) £18.50

(E) £23.76

41   The average salary of an electrician at a car manufacturer is £44,500 and is due to rise in line with inflation of 3% a year over the next three years. What is the electrician's average salary in three years' time?

(A) £45,835

(B) £47,626

(C) £48,505

(D) £48,626

(E) £48,835

42   Demand for office rental property in an office block fell by a quarter during 2008. If it was 82% full at the start of 2008 what was the percentage occupancy by the end of 2008?

(A) 615%

(B) 61.5%

(C) 56%

(D) 5.6%

(E) 6.15%

43 A sales rep spends one fifth of his time travelling and a third of this time meeting clients. In a typical 30-hour week, how many hours approximately does this sales rep spend on other tasks (apart from travelling and meeting clients)?

(A) 14

(B) 12

(C) 11

(D) 9

(E) 7

44 A consultancy's operating costs to turnover ratio is 3 : 20 each year. If the company's turnover is £213,250 in Year 1, £268,460 in Year 2 and £328,915 in Year 3, what are the total operating costs for the three-year period to the nearest £?

(A) £121,594

(B) £211,694

(C) £328,915

(D) £528,894

(E) £810,625

45 An expenses budget of £640 is spread amongst seven teams, although one team gets twice as much as the others who each receive an equal amount. How much do the other six teams receive each?

(A) Can't say

(B) £60

(C) £70

(D) £80

(E) £90

46 Of the 42 staff employed by a market research company in a ratio of 2 : 1 at two sites, the workforce at the company's

smaller site is to be cut by a half. What fraction of total staff does this reduction represent?

(A) ⅑

(B) ⅛

(C) ⅐

(D) ⅙

(E) ⅕

47 Advertising spend by a utility company is predicted to grow by £125,000 a year. If the current advertising spend is £725,000 then what will the advertising spend be in five years' time?

(A) £125,000

(B) £135,000

(C) £1,250,000

(D) £1,350,000

(E) £1,400,000

Use the figures provided in the graph *Oil demand 2008 (million barrels per day) for five countries* to answer questions 48–51.

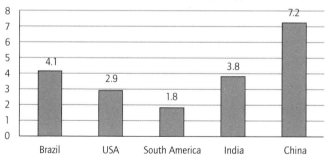

Oil demand 2008 (million barrels per day)

48 What is the ratio of South American to Chinese oil demand?

(A) 1 : 2

(B) 1 : 3

(C) 1 : 4

(D) 1 : 5

(E) 1 : 6

49 Which of the countries shown will have an oil demand in 2009 in excess of 4.4 million barrels per day if each country experiences a 15% increase in oil demand from 2008 to 2009?

(A) None of these

(B) USA, China, India and Brazil

(C) China

(D) Brazil and China

(E) China, India and Brazil

50 Oil demand in 2009 decreases 24% across each country. Put the countries in order of their decreasing oil demand.

(A) China, Brazil, USA, India, South America

(B) Brazil, China, India, USA, South America

(C) China, Brazil, India, South America, USA

(D) China, India, Brazil, USA, South America

(E) China, Brazil, India, USA, South America

51 Which three countries combined have an oil demand of 8.8 million barrels per day in 2008?

(A) Brazil, USA, South America

(B) India, USA, South America

(C) China, India, South America

(D) China, Europe, India

(E) China, USA, South America

52 The carbon dioxide emission rate for the average car is 145 g/km. How much carbon dioxide (to the nearest kg) would be emitted over a 145 km journey?

(A) 21 kg

(B) 19 kg

(C) 17 kg

(D) 15 kg

(E) 12 kg

53 The market for online advertising in the UK is estimated to be worth £3.2 billion. The error band for this is one twen-

tieth higher and one twentieth lower. What are the lower and higher estimates of the online advertising market?

(A) £3.02 billion – £3.34 billion

(B) £3.04 billion – £3.36 billion

(C) £3.06 billion – £3.38 billion

(D) £3.08 billion – £3.40 billion

(E) £3.10 billion – £3.42 billion

To answer questions 54–57 use the graph *Dairy producer sales (£10,000s) for milk and cheese between 2004 and 2008.*

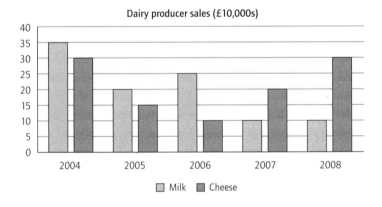

54 The projected milk sales for 2009 are 1.08 times higher than those of 2008. What would this make the total milk sales between 2005 and 2009 (in £10,000s)?

(A) 75.08

(B) 88.00

(C) 90.08

(D) 95.08

(E) 105.00

55 In which two years was there the same combined production of cheese and milk?

(A) 2004 and 2006

(B) 2005 and 2006

(C) 2006 and 2007

(D) 2007 and 2008

(E) 2008 and 2004

56 What were the average annual cheese sales across the five years shown?

(A) 200,000

(B) 205,000

(C) 210,000

(D) 215,000

(E) 220,000

57 In which year was there the greatest difference between cheese and milk sales?

(A) 2004

(B) 2005

(C) 2006

(D) 2007

(E) 2008

58 An IT consultancy company pays 8% of its total annual costs on rent and 74% on salaries. If its total annual costs are £620,000, what is the total of the other costs (excluding rent and salaries)?

(A) £49,600

(B) £99,200

(C) £111,600

(D) £229,400

(E) £458,800

To answer questions 59–62 use the graph *Half-yearly sales figures (£10,000s) for years 1 to 5*.

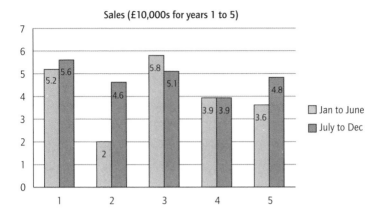

Sales (£10,000s for years 1 to 5)

59 What is the difference in the total sales for years 1–2 and
    years 3–5 (in £10,000s)?
    (A) 8.7
    (B) 9.7
    (C) 10.7
    (D) 87
    (E) 97

60 In an audit the Year 3 sales are discovered to be 4% too
    high. What is the correct figure (to the nearest £1,000)?
    (A) £94,000
    (B) £104,000
    (C) £105,000
    (D) £114,000
    (E) £115,000

61 In which year was the half-yearly sales greater between
    January and June than between July and December?
    (A) Year 1
    (B) Year 2
    (C) Year 3
    (D) Year 4
    (E) Year 5

62 In which year was there an increase in January–June sales compared to the previous year?

(A) Year 1

(B) Year 2

(C) Year 3

(D) Year 4

(E) Year 5

63 The current year's UK earnings for an airline operator are predicted to be 15% less than last year's £4.85 million. The current year's US earnings are predicted to be 25% more than last year's £10.3 million. What is the difference in earnings predicted to be between the UK and US (to the nearest million)?

(A) £5 million

(B) £6 million

(C) £7 million

(D) £8 million

(E) £9 million

64 The market share of a leading CD retail chain is 28.4%. Its two main rivals have 14.2% and 10.8% of the market share respectively. Given a total market size of €53 million, what is the value of the market outside these three retailers (to the nearest million Euros)?

(A) 25

(B) 26

(C) 27

(D) 28

(E) 29

65 A worldwide tour operator has 3,500 employees. There is an average of 250 employees in each of the eight European countries where it operates. What fraction of employees work in Europe?

(A) ½

(B) ²⁄₇

(C) ³⁄₇

(D) ⁴⁄₇

(E) ⁵⁄₇

Use the figures provided in the table *UK imports and exports for quarters 1 to 4 (£ millions)* to answer questions 66–68.

UK import and exports for quarters 1 to 4 (£ millions)

	Quarter 1	Quarter 2	Quarter 3	Quarter 4
UK imports (£ millions)	71,347	67,780	64,391	61,171
UK exports (£ millions)	63,682	66,866	70,209	73,720

66 If the percentage increase between Quarter 3 and 4 is the same for the next quarter, what will the next quarter's UK exports be approximately (to the nearest £1,000 million)?

(A) £67,000 million

(B) £77,000 million

(C) £87,000 million

(D) £97,000 million

(E) £107,000 million

67 Put the quarters in order of increasing difference between UK imports and exports.

(A) Quarter 4, Quarter 3, Quarter 2, Quarter 1

(B) Quarter 1, Quarter 3, Quarter 2, Quarter 4

(C) Quarter 4, Quarter 2, Quarter 3, Quarter 1

(D) Quarter 1, Quarter 2, Quarter 4, Quarter 3

(E) Quarter 4, Quarter 1, Quarter 3, Quarter 2

68 Which of the following statements is true?

(A) The total imports for the year shown are £264,689 million.

(B) The total exports for the year shown are £265,000 million.

(C) The highest level of exports was in Quarter 1.

(D) The trend is for increasing imports and increasing exports.

(E) The trend is for increasing imports and decreasing exports.

To answer questions 69–72 refer to graph *Quarterly sales (£10,000s) for 2005–2008*.

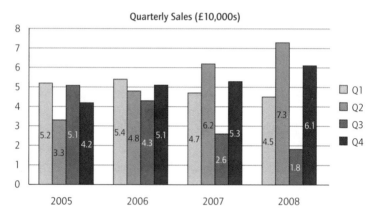

Quarterly Sales (£10,000s)

69 If the total cost of sales in 2008 was £87,000 what was the profit (where profit = total sales − total cost of sales)

(A) £197,000

(B) £190,000

(C) £117,000

(D) £110,000

(E) £107,000

70 What was the overall percentage increase in 4th quarter sales between years 2005 and 2008 (to the nearest %)?

(A) 45%

(B) 50%

(C) 54%

(D) 55%

(E) 65%

71 In which year and which quarter was there the lowest quarterly sales?

(A) Q2 2005

(B) Q3 2007

(C) Q1 2008

(D) Q3 2008

(E) Q2 2008

72 Between which two quarters was there the largest change in sales?

(A) Q3–Q4 2006

(B) Q3–Q4 2007

(C) Q3–Q4 2008

(D) Q2–Q3 2008

(E) Q2–Q3 2006

73 A broadband provider has two packages: one costs £24.00 per month, the other an extra £5.00 per month for a super-fast broadband option. What is the annual difference in cost between the two packages?

(A) No difference

(B) £40.00

(C) £50.00

(D) £60.00

(E) £70.00

74 A paint producer sells two-litre pots of paint (cost £9.25 each) and half-litre pots of paint (cost £3.50). A customer estimates that he needs 3.5 litres of paint to paint his garage. Assuming the customer minimises his costs, how much will he spend on paint?

(A) £9.00

(B) £9.25

(C) £18.50

(D) £19.75

(E) £23.25

75 A company profit and loss account contains the following operating costs: infrastructure (£2.1 million); transport (£2.8 million); and salaries (£7.7 million). What is the ratio between the operating costs for infrastructure, transport and salaries?

(A) 3:4:11

(B) 2.8:2.1:7.7

(C) None of these

(D) 28:77:21

(E) 7:8:1

76 Sales team A makes sales of £92,500, £69,000, £115,600 and £89,000 for Quarters 1–4 respectively. If there were 15 members in this team, what sales is each salesperson making on average per month (to the nearest £)?

(A) £2,034

(B) £16,474

(C) £32,949

(D) £43,932

(E) £65,898

To answer questions 77–79 refer to the graph *Clothes shop sales for brands A, B and C January to May.*

Clothes shop sales (£10,000s)

77   Which months have seen consecutive increases in both brand A and brand B sales?
(A) Jan, Feb
(B) Feb, March
(C) March, April
(D) April, May
(E) None of these

78   In which months were the total sales in excess of £166,000?
(A) April and May
(B) March and April
(C) March, April and May
(D) March and April
(E) None of these

79   In which month was the ratio of sales from Brands A : B : C in the ratio 4 : 3 : 1?
(A) January
(B) February
(C) March
(D) April
(E) May

Answer explanations

1   £212 million × ¼ = £53 million
£40 million × ³⁰⁄₁₀₀ = £12 million
£53 million − £12 million = £41 million
The correct answer is (D) £41 million higher

2    $480,000 + $440,000 = $920,000
$920,000 / $1,150,000 = 920/1150 = ⅘
The correct answer is (E) ⅘

3    $950 million + $178 million = $1,128 million
$1,128 million / $9,400 million × 100% = 12%
The correct answer is (D) 12%

4   $£48,000 : £64,000 = 3 : 4$
    The correct answer is (C) $3 : 4$

5   $£319,000$ million $- £234,000$ million $= £85$ million
    $£85$ million $/ £234,000$ million $\times 100\% = 36.3\%$
    The correct answer is (D) 36.3%

6   $100\% - 60\% = 40\%$ of employees did not complete the survey
    $225 \times {}^{40}/_{100} = 90$ employees
    The correct answer is (C) 90

7   Calculate the value of each pension fund. Use the share value of $£3.25$ provided in the table. Work your way down the list until you get to the correct answer.
    Pension fund A value $= £3.25 \times 40,500 = £131,625.00$
    Pension fund B value $= £3.25 \times 36,750 = £119,437.50$
    Pension fund C value $= £3.25 \times 25,400 = £82,550.00$
    The correct answer is (C) Pension fund C

8   40,500 shares $= 20.25\%$
    $100\% = 40,500 \times 100 / 20.25 = 200,000$
    The correct answer is (D) 200,000
    (Alternatively, $82,550 / 3.25 = 25,400$ i.e. pension fund C)

9   Carry on where we left off with question 7; calculating the value of each pension fund.
    Pension fund A value $= £131,625.00$
    Pension fund B value $= £119,437.50$
    Pension fund C value $= £82,550.00$
    Pension fund D value $= £72,475$
    Pension fund E value $= £59,312.50$
    Average $=$ Total $/ 5 = £465,400 / 5 = £93,080$
    The correct answer is (A) $£93,000$ (to the nearest $£1,000$)

10 The correct answer is (A) Can't tell because you need to know the number of employees in order to do the calculation.

! brilliant warning

Be wary of spending too much time on such trick questions. If you do not see a way of working it out then the Can't tell answer option is the one that you need.

---

11   Finance Director's total annual package = 100% + 35% = 135%
$\pounds360,000 \times 135 / 100 = \pounds486,000$
The correct answer is (C) $\pounds486,000$

12   Let washing machine brand B sales = x
Washing machine brand A sales = 3x
$3x + x = \pounds440,000$
$4x = \pounds440,000$
$x = \pounds440,000 / 4 = \pounds110,000$
The correct answer is (B) $\pounds110,000$

13   Average amount of imported coal over the 5 years shown = (60 + 55 + 40 + 35 + 45) / 5 = 235 / 5 = 47
The correct answer is (C) 47 million tonnes

14   Divide the imported coal by the indigenous coal for each year.
Year 1 = 60 / 170 = 0.35
Year 2 = 55 / 180 = 0.31
Year 3 = 40 / 175 = 0.23
Year 4 = 35 / 190 = 0.18
Year 5 = 45 / 182 = 0.25
The correct answer is (D) Year 4

15   Year 2 is clearly the highest and Year 3 the lowest. Then, calculate the totals to rank order the other three years (Years 1, 4 and 5):
Year 1 = 230 million tonnes

Year 4 = 225 million tonnes
Year 5 = 227 million tonnes
Putting these years in order of decreasing total coal demand
the correct answer is (A); Year 2, Year 1, Year 5, Year 4, Year 3

16   The correct answer is (C) Years 3–4.

brilliant tip

This question could be answered without doing the actual
calculations; it is clear that the largest change in indigenous supply
is the increase from 175 to 190 million tonnes between Years 3
and 4.

17   This requires you to work out cumulative interest.

brilliant warning

Do not simply add up 4% + 5% + 4.5% = 13.5% and then work out
13.5% of £2.15 million to be £2.44 million. This approach will lead you
incorrectly to distracter answer option B. It's close to the actual answer but
it's still wrong!

£2.15 million × 104 / 100 = £2.23 million
£2.23 million × 105 / 100 = £2.34 million
£2.34 million × 104.5 / 100 = £2.45 million
The correct answer is (C) £2.45 million

18   Note firstly that
Profit = total sales − total cost
Note secondly that the calculation needs to be in litres
throughout
Milk quantity sold (in litres) = 2,500 gallons × 4.546 / 2
So, total sales (of 2,500 gallons of milk) = £1.05 × (2,500
× 4.546 / 2) = £5,966.63

Total cost (using litres of milk) = 24.5p × 2,500 × 4.546
= £2,784.43
Profit = total sales − total cost = £5,966.63 − £2,784.43
= £3,182.20
The correct answer is (B) £3,182 (to the nearest £)

19 11 × 4.5 × (91.5 − 85.2p) = £3.12 (rounded to 2 decimal places).
The correct answer is (A) £3.12

20 £96,000 × 125 / 100 = £120,000
The correct answer is (E) £120,000

21 (500 × $1,390) − (500 × $950) = ($1,390 − $950) × 500
= $220,000
The correct answer is (A) $220,000

22 Calculate total budget cut for next year
(900 × 5%) + (1,350 × 12%) + (400 × 7.5%) + (750 × 8%) + (1,500 × 12.5%)
= 45 + 162 + 30 + 60 + 187.5
= $484.50
Exchange rate = $1.46
$484.50 / 1.46 = 331.8
The correct answer is (B) £332 (to the nearest £)

23 You can use the individual calculations for question 22.
The correct answer is (E) None of these

24 Using the calculations from question 22 again; total cut = $484.50
Current budget total = $900 + $1,350 + $400 + $750 + $1,500 = $4,900
100 × $484.50 / $4,900 = 9.9%
The correct answer is (A) 9.9%

25 12.5 / 100 = 1 / 8
The correct answer is (A) ⅛

26 For two weeks the sales are £5,500 × 2 = £11,000
For another two weeks the sales = 2 × £5,500 × 105% /
100 = £11,550
Total monthly sales = £11,000 + £11,550 = £22,550
The correct answer is (E) £22,550

27 A quick review of the table will reveal those three regions
where sales decreased between 2006 and 2008.
The correct answer is (C) a, b, e

28 Calculate the percentage change in sales value for each
region between 2007 and 2008.
Note that the question specifies 2007 – not 2006 (the first
column shown in the table)
Region a = (1.29 − 1.64) / 1.64 = 21.3% decrease
Region b = (0.31 − 0.52) / 0.52 = 40.4% decrease
Region c = (5.91 − 6.11) / 6.11 = 3.3% decrease
Region d = (5.88 − 5.86) / 5.88 = 0.34% increase
Region e = (2.05 − 2.79) / 2.79 = 26.5% decrease
The correct answer is (B) Region b

29 A quick review of the table will reveal which region was the
highest regional performer in 2006, 2007 and 2008.
The correct answer is (C) Region c

30 6.2p × 3,250 shares = £201.50
The correct answer is (A) £201.50

brilliant tips

- Question 29 is easy so don't spend too long double-checking
  your answer and wasting time thinking that there must be more
  to it. Sometimes if it seems too good to be true it actually is!

- Question 30 is another simple calculation – don't be put off by
  the use of business language in the question, such as interim
  dividend or per share.

31 Looking at the line graph you can see that there are three months when office paper demand is higher than supply. Month 4 clearly has the largest gap between the two lines on the graph. (The difference = 844 − 605 although you may not need to work this out.)

The correct answer is (D) Month 4

32 Total difference between supply and demand = Total supply − total demand = 3,580− 3,579 = 1

The correct answer is (A) 1 tonne

33 Starting with the first month; calculating the difference between supply and demand gives you the answer straight away

745 − 642 = 103 tonnes

The correct answer is (A) Month 1

34 The correct answer is (B) 2 months

35 £143,850 = 21%

100% = 100 × 143,850 / 21 = 685,000

The correct answer is (E) 685 (in £1000s)

36 £4.6 million × 65 / 100 = £2.99 million

The correct answer is (B) 29.90 (in £100,000s)

---

brilliant tip

Beware of going for the distracter answer option of 2.99 which would be the answer (in £ millions).

---

37 The question asks about the difference in passenger numbers (not whether there has been an increase or decrease).

January difference = 28,000

February difference = 81,000

March difference = 35,000

April difference = 16,000
May difference = 38,000
June difference = 26,000
Greatest difference = February
Second greatest difference = May
The correct answer is (E) May

38   French monthly sales = €60,600
German sales = €20,200
Spanish sales = €20,200
Total sales across the three European countries (in Euros)
= 60,600 + 20,200 + 20,200
The correct answer is (A) €101,000

39   42.6 million / 1.4 = £30.43 million
The correct answer is (D) £30.43 million

40   €6.6 × 3 = €19.8
19.8 / 1.2 = 16.50
The correct answer is (C) £16.50

41   Year 1 increase = £44,500 × 103 / 100 = £45,835
Year 2 increase = £45,835 × 103 / 100 = £47,210
Year 3 increase = £47,210 × 103 / 100 = £48,626
The correct answer is (D) £48,626

brilliant tips

- On question 40 make sure whenever using exchange rates that you divide (or multiply) in the right direction. It's best to personalise it and/or to visualise how much money you would expect to have in your hands. There are 1.2 Euros to the £ so you get less £ for each Euro that you have ... so the answer in £ must be lower than the answer in Euros.

- On question 41 remember to use compound interest each year. Otherwise you could end up being misled and go for the £48,505 answer option (£44,500 × 109%).

42   82% × 3 / 4 = 61.5%
The correct answer is (B) 61.5%

43   ⅕ + ⅓ = ³⁄₁₅ + ⁵⁄₁₅ = ⁸⁄₁₅
1 − ⁸⁄₁₅ = ⁷⁄₁₅
⁷⁄₁₅ × 30-hour week = 14 hours
The correct answer is (A) 14

44   Total costs = £213,250 + £268,460 + £328,915 = £810,625
Operating costs = 3 / 20 × £810,625 = £121,593.75
The correct answer is (A) £121,594

45   Let x = amount that each team gets
2x + 6x = 640
x = 640 / 8 = 80
The correct answer is (D) £80

46   42 staff in a 2 : 1 ratio means that 14 staff work at one site and 28 staff at the other site.
So, cutting the workforce at the company's smaller site by 50% = 7 staff
⁷⁄₄₂ = ⅙
The correct answer is (D) ⅙

47   £725,000 + (5 × £125,000) = £1,350,000
The correct answer is (D) £1,350,000

48   Ratio of South American to Chinese oil demand = 1.8 : 7.2
= 1 : 4
The correct answer is (C) 1 : 4

49   The correct answer is (D) Brazil and China

> ### ✸ **brilliant** tip
>
> This is one of those questions where you can easily eliminate
> answer options. Before doing any calculations you can tell just from
> looking at the graph that there are only three countries in
> contention:
>
> … You know that China has to be in the answer (oil demand = 7.2)
>
> … You then need to calculate which of Brazil and India qualify:
>
> Brazil; 4.1 × 115 / 100 = 4.715
>
> India; 3.8 × 115 / 100 = 4.37

50　The 24% decrease across each country is an irrelevancy.
The same percentage decrease applies across all the coun-
tries. Hence the relative order of decreasing oil demand
remains the same as shown in the graph.
The correct answer is (E) China, Brazil, India, USA, South
America

51　The correct answer is (A) Brazil, USA, South America

> ### ✸ **brilliant** tip
>
> You should be able to work out in your head which combinations of
> three countries will add up to 8.8 million barrels per day. You can
> exclude China's 7.2 million barrels per day straight away since its
> contribution would make it too high to be included (once two other
> countries were added in).

52　145 × 145 g = 21,025 g
1000 g = 1 kg
So 21,025 g = 21.025 kg
The correct answer is (A) 21 kg to the nearest kg

53 £3.2 billion × 95 / 100 = £3.04 billion
£3.2 billion × 105 / 100 = £3.36 billion
The correct answer is (B) £3.04 billion – £3.36 billion

54 First you need to calculate the total milk sales for 2005
(note not 2004) to 2008

brilliant tip

Ignore the £10,000s since this will be constant throughout your
calculation.

20 + 25 + 10 + 10 = 65
2009 sales = 10 × 108 / 100 = 10.08
Total milk sales 2005–2009 = 65 + 10.08 = 75.08
The correct answer is (A) 75.08

55 You can exclude 2004 just from looking at the graph; both
milk and cheese sales are higher than any other year
2005 cheese and milk sales = 20 + 15 = 35
2006 cheese and milk sales = 25 + 10 = 35
2007 cheese and milk sales = 10 + 20 = 30
2008 cheese and milk sales = 10 + 30 = 40
The correct answer is (B) 2005 and 2006

56 Average annual cheese sales across the five years shown =
30 + 15 + 10 + 20 + 30 = 1,050,000
1,050,000 / 5 = 210,000
The correct answer is (C); 210,000

57 You need to look for the largest gap between the cheese and
milk sales on the graph.
The correct answer is (E) 2008

58 8% + 74% = 82% on rent and salary costs
Total annual costs = £620,000 = 100%
Total of other costs (excluding rent and salaries) = 18% of
£620,000

£620,000 × 18 / 100 = £111,600
The correct answer is (C) £111,600

59 Total sales for years 1–2 = 5.2 + 2 + 5.6 + 4.6 = 17.4
Total sales for years 3–5 = 5.8 + 5.1 + 3.9 + 3.9 + 3.6 + 4.8 = 27.1
Difference = 27.1 − 17.4 = 9.7
The correct answer is (B) 9.7

60 Year 3 sales − 4% = (5.8 + 5.1) × 96 / 100 = £104,640
The correct answer is (C) £105,000

61 Look at the graph to see where the January–June figures are above the July– December figures.
The correct answer is (C) Year 3

62 Look at the graph to see where there has been an increase in January–June sales
The correct answer is (C) Year 3

63 The current year's UK earnings for an airline operator are predicted to be 15% less than last year's
UK earnings; £4.85 million × 85 / 100 = £4.1225 million
US earnings; £10.3 million × 125 / 100 = £12.875 million
Difference in earnings predicted between the UK and US = £12.875 million − £4.1225 million = £8.7525 million
To the nearest million; £8.7525 million = £9 million
The correct answer is (E) £9 million

64 28.4% + 14.2% + 10.8% = 53.4%
100% = €53 million
Value of the market outside these three retailers = 100% − 53.4% = 46.6%
46.6 / 100 × €53 million = €24.7 million
The correct answer is (A) 25 (to the nearest million Euros)

65 250 × 8 = 2000
2000 / 3500 = 4/7
The correct answer is (D) 4/7

66 Percentage increase between Quarter 3 and 4 = (73,720 −
70,209) / 70,209 = 5%
So, applying the same 5% increase for the next quarter =
73,720 × 105 / 100 = 77,406
77,406 to the nearest 1,000 = 77,000
The correct answer is (B) £77,000 million

67 The correct answer is (E) Quarter 4, Quarter 1, Quarter 3,
Quarter 2
Calculate the difference between UK imports and exports
for each quarter
Quarter 1 = 71,347 − 63,682 = 7,665
Quarter 2 = 67,780 − 66,866 = 914
Quarter 3 = 64,391 − 70,209 = −5,819
Quarter 4 = 61,171 − 73,720 = −12,549

68 The correct answer is (A) The total imports for the year
shown are £264,689 million.

brilliant approaches

- On question 67 note that the question asks only about the
  difference (so whether there has been an increase or decrease is
  irrelevant).

- To find the true statement in question 68 start by briefly
  reviewing them all. Do any look as though they could be false?
  Do any look as though they could be true? Start by eliminating
  those that look the easiest to check, e.g. 'The trend is for
  increasing imports and decreasing exports' and 'The trend is for
  increasing imports and increasing exports' can be disproved by
  looking at the Table and seeing that imports are on a
  decreasing trend with exports on an increasing trend. Since
  exports are increasing each quarter, 'The highest level of
  exports was in Quarter 1' is false. Thus, 'The total exports for
  the year shown is £265,000 million' is false. Total imports for
  the year = 71,347 + 67,780 + 64,391 + 61,171 = 264,689.

69   Profit = total sales − total cost of sales (£87,000)
Total sales = £45,000 + £73,000 + £18,000 + £61,000
= £197,000
Profit = £197,000 − £87,000 = £110,000
The correct answer is (D) £110,000

70   100% × (6.1 − 4.2) / 4.2 = 45.2%
The correct answer is (A) 45%

71   Review the graph to see where there is the lowest value.
Then read off the year and the quarter.
The correct answer is (D) Q3 2008

72   Review the graph to see where there have been large
increases or decreases in sales.
Work out the value of those that could be the largest shown,
e.g.
Q2–Q3 2007 = 6.2 − 2.6 = 3.6
Q3–Q4 2007 = 5.3 − 2.6 = 2.7
Q2–Q3 2008 = 7.3 − 1.8 = 5.5
Q3–Q4 2008 = 6.1 − 1.8 = 4.3
The correct answer is (D) Q2–Q3 2008

73   Package 1 = £24.00 × 12 = £288.00 a year
Package 2 = (£24.00 + £5.00) × 12 = £348.00 a year
Annual difference in cost between the two packages = £348
− £288 = £60
The correct answer is (D) £60.00

74   Cost two 2-litre pots 2 × £9.25 = £18.50
The correct answer is (C) £18.50

75 Infrastructure (£2.1 million) : transport (£2.8 million) : salaries (£7.7 million)

= 2.1 : 2.8 : 7.7

= 3 : 4 : 11

The correct answer is (A) 3 : 4 : 11

76 Total sales of team A = £92,500 + £69,000 + £115,600 + £89,000 = £366,100

Average per sales person = £366,100 / 15 = £24,407

Average per sales person per month = £24,407 / 12 = £2,034

The correct answer is (A) £2,034

77 Review the graph to see where there has been a consecutive increase in sales for brand A. Then see if for those months there has also been a consecutive increase in sales for brand B sales.

The correct answer is (C) March, April

78 Calculate the total sales for each month

January; 6.2 + 2 + 4 = 12.2

February; 5.6 + 4.6 + 5.1 = 15.3

March; 7.1 + 6.2 + 3.6 = 16.9

April; 10 + 7.75 + 2.25 = 20

May; 8 + 4.3 + 4.3 = 16.6

Total sales were in excess of £16,600 in March and April
The correct answer is (B); March and April

79   Review the graphs for a 4 : 3 : 1 pattern i.e. Brand A is 4
     times the size of Brand C; and Brand B is 3 times the size
     of Brand C.
     The correct answer is (D); April

CHAPTER 10

Senior-management level numeracy tests

You may be wondering why you need to take a numeracy test if you have already proven yourself in a business environment. However, finding the right person for a job is always important, and never more so than at the senior management level when an inappropriate selection can be a costly and time-consuming mistake. That's why organisations use objective numeracy tests to assess candidates' high-level numerical reasoning skills and sift out unsuitable applicants for top jobs.

When are they taken?

Senior-level numeracy tests are almost always given in a recruitment context. Often, the numeracy test is just one component of an assessment centre, which may also include verbal reasoning tests, an interview, and role-play and group exercises. These sorts of tests may also be used as part of a development centre whereby internal candidates are assessed for promotional opportunities within their organisation.

How are they taken?

These tests are available in both pencil-and-paper and online formats. Senior managerial numeracy tests usually contain about 30–40 questions and have a time limit ranging from about 30 to 40 minutes. You will be able to use a calculator to answer the questions.

What do they look like?

You will be presented with several tables and graphs of data alongside several associated multiple-choice questions. You then need to decide which graph/s or table/s contain(s) the data that you need. There are no text-only questions. As per the graduate-level questions, you can expect to receive a range of graphs, from bar charts to pie charts. But the graphs that you need to analyse and numerical data that you need to use will be more complex than those found in earlier chapters of this book. You will usually need to refer to more than one source of data to reach your answer.

The questions are designed to mirror the type of numerical problems that managers face in the workplace and are set within an organisational context. So you are being assessed on applying your numeracy skills to business data. Many of the practice questions are set within the context of a (fictitious) international company, called *Conglomerate plc*. But remember, it is the figures not the setting that you need to focus on.

How hard are they?

These are the most difficult questions in the book. You have been warned! Although these questions share a similar format with the graduate-level questions in the previous chapter, this range is benchmarked at a higher level. That said, there are many different senior managerial numeracy tests on the market, and they vary in difficulty level. These questions take longer since there are often two or more calculations to conduct for each question. They are not necessarily complex calculations. But as the number of calculations increases so does the opportunity for error. In fact, senior managerial questions are assessing how accurately you can work your way through the multiple stages of a maths calculation.

Instructions

Start off by deciding what data you need and which of the graphs and/or tables contains it. Bear in mind that for the more difficult questions you will need to relate figures across two graphs and/or tables. Then locate the specific data that you need. Always think through what the question is saying before diving into the calculation. You might be able to arrive at an answer without actually doing a calculation just by studying trends in the graph.

It's hard to provide guidance on time limits with these questions, as different people will find different things difficult. If possible, be sure to pick off the easiest questions first! Aim to spend just over a minute per question but be aware that some questions will take considerably longer than this to answer.

brilliant tips

- Keep things simple whenever possible. Focus on the one-to-nine digits in each figure rather than the zeros (tens, hundreds, thousands, millions even) that come after the digits. Avoid worrying about the zeros in every part of your calculation. You can just ignore the scale of the figures that you are working with, for example millions or tens of millions. These will be standard in both question and answer. You can also simplify matters by working to one decimal point in your calculation, thus cutting down on the number of figures that you need to write down and manipulate.

- Don't go for an answer just because it is the closest to your own calculation. The question will specify if you need to round up an answer.

Practice questions

Use the figures provided in the two tables and graph to answer questions 1–5.

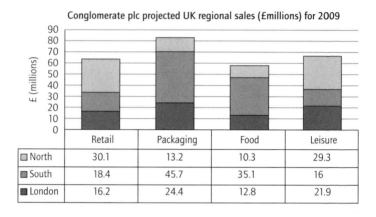

Conglomerate plc projected UK regional sales (£millions) for 2009

	Retail	Packaging	Food	Leisure
North	30.1	13.2	10.3	29.3
South	18.4	45.7	35.1	16
London	16.2	24.4	12.8	21.9

Conglomerate plc turnover by world region

	2006 (£ millions)	2007 (£ millions)	2008 (£ millions)
Asia-Pacific	280.8	282.3	292.2
UK	479.3	482.5	477.9
North America	341	352.7	364.5
South America	180.3	133.9	86.7
Rest of World	139.2	162.2	174.7
Total	1420.6	1413.6	1396.0

Conglomerate plc worldwide turnover by market sector

	2006 (£ millions)	2007 (£ millions)	2008 (£ millions)
Retail	314.5	318.2	321.9
Leisure markets	173.1	164.6	161.8
Packaging	469.2	474.9	467.6
Food markets	411.6	403.1	392.3
Other markets	52.2	52.8	52.4
Total	1420.6	1413.6	1396.0

1   How many world regions and market sectors have shown an annual turnover increase in both 2007 and 2008?
    (A) 1 world region; 1 market sector
    (B) 1 world region; 2 market sectors
    (C) 2 world regions; 1 market sector
    (D) 2 world regions; 2 market sectors
    (E) 3 world regions; 1 market sector

2   Which market sector and which world region have shown the lowest absolute change between 2006 and 2008?
    (A) South America, Retail
    (B) Asia-Pacific, Packaging
    (C) Other markets, Packaging
    (D) UK, Other markets
    (E) UK, Packaging

3   What are the total projected sales for 2009 in the Northern and Southern regions?
    (A) £140.5 million
    (B) £158.2 million
    (C) £190.5 million
    (D) £198.1 million
    (E) £273.4 million

4   What approximate percentage change in UK regional sales is predicted from 2008 to 2009?
    (A) None of these
    (B) 43% decrease
    (C) 43% increase
    (D) 75% decrease
    (E) 75% increase

5   What is the absolute difference (in £ millions) between the highest and the lowest performing market sector between 2006 and 2008?
    (A) £7.4 million
    (B) £19.3 million

(C) £26.7 million

(D) £29.3 million

(E) £30.7 million

Use the figures provided in the tables, graph and pie chart to answer questions 6–10.

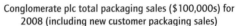

Conglomerate plc total packaging sales ($100,000s) for
2008 (including new customer packaging sales)

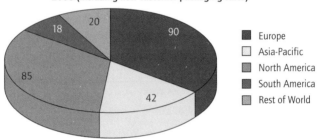

Conglomerate plc operational source

	New customer packaging sales for 2008 ($100,000s)
Asia-Pacific	7.2
Europe	5.3
North America	4.2
South America	8.1
Rest of World	3.5

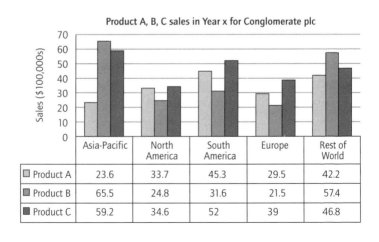

Product A, B, C sales in Year x for Conglomerate plc

	Asia-Pacific	North America	South America	Europe	Rest of World
Product A	23.6	33.7	45.3	29.5	42.2
Product B	65.5	24.8	31.6	21.5	57.4
Product C	59.2	34.6	52	39	46.8

6   The worldwide target for Product A sales is $18 million. From sales levels in Year x, by how much approximately do Product A sales need to increase to reach this target?

(A) $20,000

(B) $200,000

(C) $0.4 million

(D) $0.6 million

(E) $0.8 million

7   Which two world regions have combined Product A, B and C sales in Year x that are less than $22 million?

(A) Rest of World, North America

(B) Europe, South America

(C) Europe, North America

(D) North America, South America

(E) Europe, Rest of World

8   What are the total new customer packaging sales for 2008?

(A) $2.38 million

(B) $2.63 million

(C) $2.83 million

(D) $2.88 million

(E) $3.83 million

9   Which region's individual packaging sales has the highest percentage of new customer sales in 2008?

(A) Asia-Pacific

(B) Europe

(C) North America

(D) South America

(E) Rest of World

10   What is the ratio of European to Rest of World packaging sales in 2008?

(A) 2 : 9

(B) 9 : 2

(C) 1 : 9

(D) 9 : 1

(E) 4 : 1

Use the figures provided in the table and two graphs to answer questions 11–13.

Conglomerate plc employees by region

	2006	2007	2008
Asia-Pacific	1,048	1,274	1,502
Europe	6,375	6,404	6,453
North America	2,406	2,483	2,392
South America	1,558	1,486	1,415
Rest of World	1,850	1,508	1,124
Total	9,237	9,455	8,886

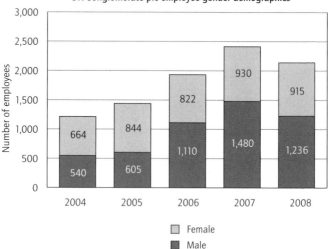

UK Conglomerate plc employee gender demographics

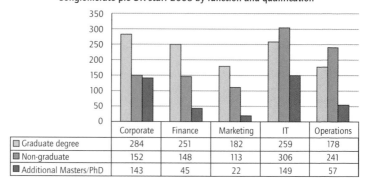

Conglomerate plc UK staff 2008 by function and qualification

	Corporate	Finance	Marketing	IT	Operations
Graduate degree	284	251	182	259	178
Non-graduate	152	148	113	306	241
Additional Masters/PhD	143	45	22	149	57

11 Which world regions show the greatest and the least change in employee numbers between 2006 and 2008?

(A) Asia-Pacific (greatest); Europe (least)

(B) Europe (greatest); North America (least)

(C) Rest of World (greatest); North America (least)

(D) North America (greatest); South America (least)

(E) Asia-Pacific (greatest); North America (least)

12 Which function has over 57% of its employees within the 'Graduate degree' group?

(A) Corporate

(B) Finance

(C) Operations

(D) IT

(E) Marketing

13 Which two years have the same ratio of male to female employees?

(A) 2004 and 2005

(B) 2006 and 2008

(C) 2005 and 2006

(D) 2007 and 2006

(E) 2004 and 2008

Use the figures provided in the three graphs to answer questions 14–18.

2008 UK sales (in £millions)

■ Online   □ Offline

	Deluxe	Supreme	Special	Extra Special
Online	25.4	23.2	24.4	27.1
Offline	32.6	23.8	15.6	24.9

Retail sales for product a (£10,000s)

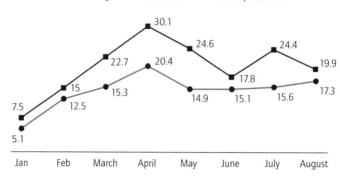

2008 sales of 4 best selling food brands in UK

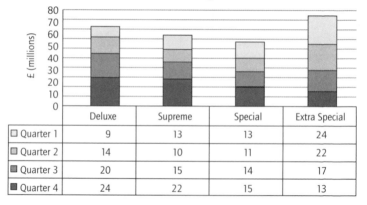

	Deluxe	Supreme	Special	Extra Special
☐ Quarter 1	9	13	13	24
☐ Quarter 2	14	10	11	22
☐ Quarter 3	20	15	14	17
■ Quarter 4	24	22	15	13

14 In which quarter were the combined sales of the Deluxe and
    Extra Special food brands the same as the combined sales
    of the Supreme and Special food brands?

   (A) Quarter 1

   (B) Quarter 2

   (C) Quarter 3

   (D) Quarter 4

   (E) Can't tell

15   In which two months is there the same difference between the high street and retail park sales for product a?
(A) January, February
(B) January, August
(C) February, August
(D) None of these
(E) April, May

16   Which products have the highest 2008 UK online and the highest overall (online and offline) sales?
(A) Can't tell
(B) Extra Special (online); Deluxe (overall)
(C) Special (online); Deluxe (overall)
(D) Deluxe (online); Extra Special (overall)
(E) Extra Special (online); Extra Special (overall)

17   In which month were high street retail sales higher than retail park sales for product a?
(A) None of these
(B) January
(C) February
(D) July
(E) August

18   Between which months did both the retail park and high street sales of Product a fall?
(A) February to March
(B) March to April
(C) April to May
(D) May to June
(E) June to July

Use the figures provided in the two tables to answer questions 19–20.

Conglomerate plc staff costs

	2006 (£100,000s)	2007 (£100,000s)	2008 (£100,000s)
Salaries	1,514.2	1,505.4	1,457.9
Social security	177.4	185.3	179.2
Pension	165.8	169.2	174.6
Bonus payments	54.2	48.7	37.3
Misc. staff costs	149.1	195.2	184.3

Conglomerate plc worldwide gross sales turnover (to year end)

	2006 (£ millions)	2007 (£ millions)	2008 (£ millions)
Retail	358.9	342.1	321.9
Packaging	162.3	164.1	161.8
Food	441.4	466.0	467.6
Leisure	358.2	377.6	392.3
Other markets	59.4	62.7	52.4

19 What was the second highest staff cost across 2006–2008?
    (A) Salaries
    (B) Social security
    (C) Pension
    (D) Bonus payments
    (E) Misc. staff costs

20 If the ratio of profit to turnover was 1 : 8 in 2007 then what
    was the profit (to the nearest £ million)?
    (A) £170 million
    (B) £177 million
    (C) £180 million
    (D) £187 million
    (E) £190 million

Use the figures provided in the two graphs to answer questions
21–23.

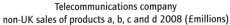

Telecommunications company
non-UK sales of products a, b, c and d 2008 (£millions)

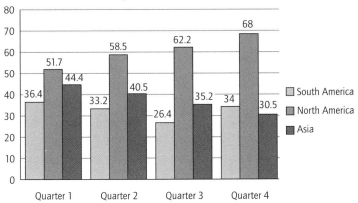

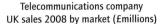

Telecommunications company
UK sales 2008 by market (£millions)

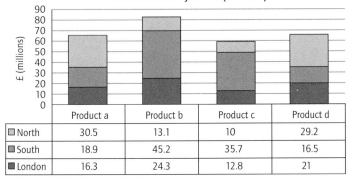

	Product a	Product b	Product c	Product d
North	30.5	13.1	10	29.2
South	18.9	45.2	35.7	16.5
London	16.3	24.3	12.8	21

21 In 2008 what is the difference between the UK and Asian
sales (to the nearest £ million)?

(A) £113 million

(B) £123 million

(C) £133 million

(D) £143 million

(E) £153 million

22 In which two quarters were the total non-UK sales the same?

(A) Quarter 1, Quarter 2

(B) Quarter 1, Quarter 3

(C) Quarter 1, Quarter 4

(D) Quarter 2, Quarter 3

(E) Quarter 3, Quarter 4

23 Due to increasing inflation, 2009's quarterly non-UK sales are predicted to be 3%, 4%, 5% and 6% higher than the respective 2008 quarters. What is the total sales prediction for 2009?

(A) £544.4 million

(B) £555.5 million

(C) £566.6 million

(D) £577.7 million

(E) £588.8 million

Use the two tables to answer questions 24–27.

Conglomerate plc UK function budgeted costs and actual costs

	Yearly budget (£100,000s)	Quarter 1 Actual cost (£100,000s)	Quarter 2 Actual cost (£100,000s)	Quarter 3 Actual cost (£100,000s)	Quarter 4 Actual cost (£100,000s)
Sales/ marketing	12	2.3	2.6	2.9	2.8
Production	35	8.8	9.5	10.1	9.1
Operations	64	15.2	15.5	16.5	17.8
Overheads	7	1.7	1.6	1.9	1.4
Rent/office expenses	24	5.9	5.8	6.4	5.7

Conglomerate plc worldwide turnover 2006–2008

	2006 (£ millions)	2007 (£ millions)	2008 (£ millions)
Retail	358.9	342.1	321.9
Packaging	162.3	164.1	161.8
Food	441.4	466.00	467.6
Leisure	358.2	377.6	392.3
Other markets	59.4	62.7	52.4
Total turnover	1,380.2	1,412.50	1,396.0

24 What is the difference between the total costs for the four quarters and the yearly budget?
    (A) £1.5 million
    (B) £1 million
    (C) £750,000
    (D) £250,000
    (E) £150,000

25 Which area's quarterly costs have the highest discrepancy with the yearly budget?
    (A) Sales/marketing
    (B) Production
    (C) Operations
    (D) Overheads
    (E) Rent/office expenses

26 Which of the following statements is true?
    (A) Quarter 1 contributed the most to the budget overspend.
    (B) Production has the highest yearly budget.
    (C) Operational costs have been increasing between quarter 1 and quarter 4.
    (D) Worldwide turnover was highest in 2008.
    (E) Worldwide turnover for all three years combined was less than £4,100 million.

27 Which of the following contributed the highest percentage to worldwide turnover between 2006 and 2008?
    (A) Retail
    (B) Packaging
    (C) Food
    (D) Leisure
    (E) Other markets

Use the figures provided in the two pie charts and table to answer questions 28–32.

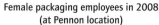

Female packaging employees in 2008
(at Pennon location)

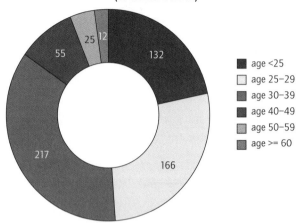

- ■ age <25
- □ age 25–29
- ■ age 30–39
- ■ age 40–49
- ■ age 50–59
- ■ age >= 60

Male packaging employees in 2008
(at Pennon location)

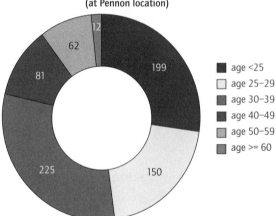

- ■ age <25
- □ age 25–29
- ■ age 30–39
- ■ age 40–49
- ■ age 50–59
- ■ age >= 60

Conglomerate plc employees by function 2006–2008

	2006	2007	2008
Retail	3,580	3,973	3,855
Logistics	1,425	1,511	1,636
Packaging	1,672	1,487	1,622
Food	1,561	1,509	1,588
Leisure	2,451	2,486	2,121
Total	10,689	10,966	10,822

28. Which function has experienced the second largest change in staff numbers between 2006 and 2008?
    (A) Retail
    (B) Logistics
    (C) Packaging
    (D) Food
    (E) Leisure

29 Which age band for packaging employees at Pennon contains the highest ratio of male to female employees?
    (A) Age <25 years
    (B) Age 25–29 years
    (C) Age 30–39 years
    (D) Age 40–49 years
    (E) Age 50–59 years

30 What is the total number of employees under 30 years of age at the Pennon location?
    (A) 367
    (B) 467
    (C) 647
    (D) 677
    (E) 766

31 If the Retail profits in 2007 are £79.46 million, what are the profits per Retail employee?
    (A) £22,000
    (B) £20,000
    (C) £19,200
    (D) £2,200
    (E) £2,000

32 In 2008 there are two Packaging sites: at Pennon and Asle. How many employees work at the Asle site?
    (A) 276
    (B) 286
    (C) 296
    (D) 306
    (E) 315

Use the figures provided in the three graphs to answer questions 33–36.

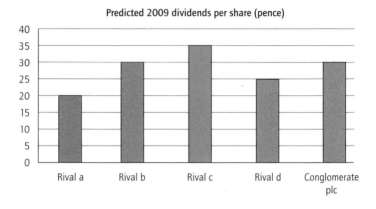

Predicted 2009 dividends per share (pence)

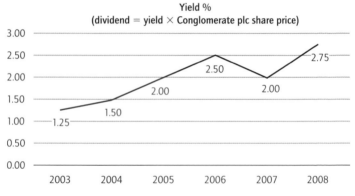

Yield %
(dividend = yield × Conglomerate plc share price)

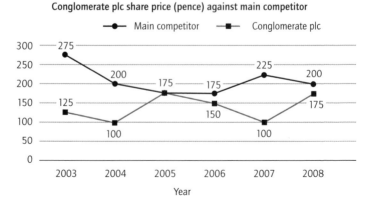

Conglomerate plc share price (pence) against main competitor

33 Over the six-year period what is the range of the price difference between the Conglomerate plc share price and its main competitor?

    (A) 0–150p

    (B) 0–125p

    (C) 0–100p

    (D) 0–75p

    (E) 0–50p

34 By what fraction does Conglomerate plc need to grow its predicted 2009 dividend to match its rival with the highest dividend?

    (A) ½

    (B) ⅓

    (C) ⅙

    (D) ⅛

    (E) ⅑

35 The predicted 2009 dividend for Conglomerate plc represents what increase per share over the 2008 dividend (to the nearest whole pence)?

    (A) 10p

    (B) 15p

    (C) 20p

    (D) 25p

    (E) Can't tell

36 How many Conglomerate plc shares would a speculator with £33,000 be able to buy at the 2006 share price?

    (A) 220,000

    (B) 22,000

    (C) 2,200

    (D) 220

    (E) 22

Use the figures provided in the three graphs to answer questions 37–40.

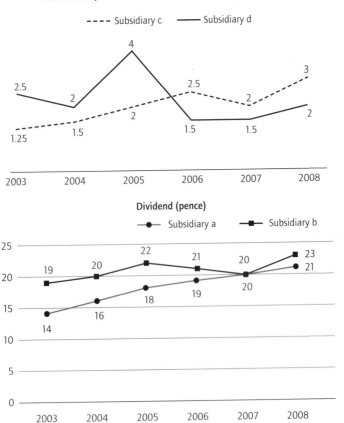

Yield x shown (where dividend = x% of subsidiary share prices)

Dividend (pence)

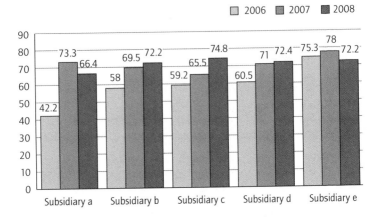

European subsidiary sales (Euros 10,000s)

37 Which subsidiary's sales were lowest in 2006 and which were highest in 2007?
   (A) Subsidiary a (2006); Subsidiary e (2007)
   (B) Subsidiary d (2006); Subsidiary e (2007)
   (C) Subsidiary a (2006); Subsidiary d (2007)
   (D) Subsidiary d (2006); Subsidiary a (2007)
   (E) Subsidiary a (2007); Subsidiary e (2006)

38 How much would a shareholder with 4,000 Subsidiary b shares have received as their dividend payment in 2004?
   (A) £700
   (B) £800
   (C) £900
   (D) £1,000
   (E) £1,100

39 When is the highest yield paid for either subsidiary c or subsidiary d between the years 2005–2008?
   (A) 2006 (Subsidiary c)
   (B) 2007 (Subsidiary c)
   (C) 2008 (Subsidiary c)
   (D) 2005 (Subsidiary d)
   (E) 2006 (Subsidiary d)

40 Between which years was there the greatest percentage change in yield for either subsidiary c or subsidiary d?
   (A) 2004–2005 (Subsidiary c)
   (B) 2004–2005 (Subsidiary d)
   (C) 2005–2006 (Subsidiary d)
   (D) 2005–2006 (Subsidiary c)
   (E) 2007–2008 (Subsidiary c)

Use the figures provided in the table, pie chart and graph to answer questions 41–45.

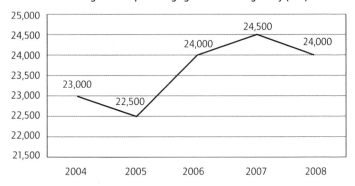

Conglomerate plc average graduate starting salary (in £)

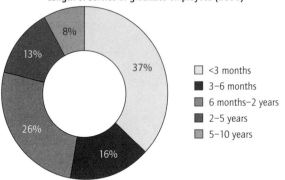

Length of service of graduate employees (2008)

Average use salary by function (2008)

Function	UK industry – Average Director salary (£1,000s)	UK industry – Average graduate starting salary (£1,000s)
Engineering/IT	78.5	24.1
Operations	74.8	23.6
Marketing	75.4	22.4
Finance	89.2	23.5
Corporate	91.5	25.1

41 If the same absolute downward trend in starting salaries between 2007 and 2008 continued between 2008 and 2009, what would the Conglomerate plc 2009 average graduate starting salary be?

(A) £24,500

(B) £24,000

(C) £23,500

(D) £23,000

(E) £22,500

42 What is the average graduate starting salary across the five years shown?

(A) £22,200

(B) £23,200

(C) £23,500

(D) £23,600

(E) £24,500

43 In which UK industry functions are there the greatest and the least difference between Director and graduate salaries?

(A) Corporate (greatest); Operations (least)

(B) Finance (greatest); Operations (least)

(C) Corporate (greatest); Marketing (least)

(D) Finance (greatest); Marketing (least)

(E) Engineering/IT (greatest); Operations (least)

44 What would the average Finance Director salary be in Euros (to the nearest 100 Euros)? Use an exchange rate of 1.12 Euros to the £.

(A) €93,900

(B) €95,900

(C) €97,900

(D) €99,900

(E) €101,900

45 If there are 2,200 graduate employees, how many have a length of service less than 6 months?
   (A) 1,166
   (B) 1,066
   (C) 814
   (D) 452
   (E) 352

Use the figures provided in the two graphs to answer questions 46–49.

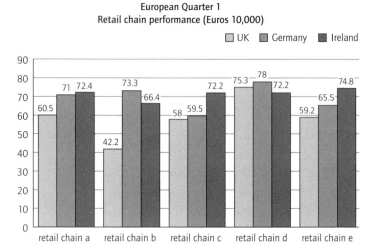

European Quarter 1
Retail chain performance (Euros 10,000)

□ UK ▨ Germany ▨ Ireland

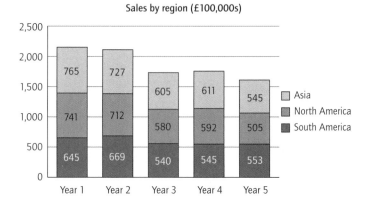

Sales by region (£100,000s)

□ Asia
▨ North America
▨ South America

46 In which year was there a greater than 10% drop in regional
    sales?
    (A) Year 1
    (B) Year 2
    (C) Year 3
    (D) Year 4
    (E) Year 5

47 Put the retail chains in order of decreasing overall sales?
    (A) Retail chains e, d, c, a, b
    (B) Retail chains d, e, c, a, b
    (C) Retail chains e, d, b, c, a
    (D) Retail chains d, e, c, b, a
    (E) Retail chains d, a, e, c, b

48 What are the total Asian sales across Years 1–5 in Euros
    using an exchange rate of 1.11 Euros to the £ (to the
    nearest million Euros)?
    (A) €361 million
    (B) €353 million
    (C) €341 million
    (D) €333 million
    (E) €323 million

49 What were the total sales for North America across the five
    years?
    (A) £313 million
    (B) £318 million
    (C) £320 million
    (D) £321 million
    (E) £323 million

Answer explanations

Each answer explanation starts by telling you which graph(s)
you need to use. The next part of the explanation then takes you
through the steps of the calculation itself.

1   Where's the information I need? Look in: *Conglomerate plc turnover by world region*; and *Conglomerate plc worldwide turnover by market sector.*

How do I calculate the answer?

Count up the number of regions and sectors that have increased between 2006 and 2007, 2007 and 2008;

Asia-Pacific, North America, Rest of World = 3 world regions

Retail = 1 market sector

So the correct answer is (E); 3 world regions; 1 market sector

2   Where's the information I need? Look in: *Conglomerate plc turnover by world region* and *Conglomerate plc worldwide turnover by market sector.*

How do I calculate the answer?

You need to calculate the difference between the 2006 and 2008 figures for each world region and each market sector.

brilliant tip

Absolute change means that you can ignore whether the change has been an increase or a decrease.

Asia-Pacific = $292.2 - 280.8 = 11.4$
UK = $477.9 - 479.3 = -1.4$
North America = $364.5 - 341 = 23.5$
South America = $180.3 - 86.7 = 93.6$
Rest of World = $174.7 - 139.2 = 35.5$
Retail = $321.9 - 314.5 = 7.4$
Leisure markets = $161.8 - 173.1 = -11.3$
Packaging = $467.6 - 469.2 = -1.6$
Food markets = $392.3 - 411.6 = -19.3$
Other markets = $52.4 - 52.2 = 0.2$
So the correct answer is (D) UK, Other markets

3   Where's the information I need? Look in: *Conglomerate plc projected UK regional sales (£ millions) for 2009.*
How do I calculate the answer?
Add the projected sales for the Northern (£82.9 million) and the Southern regions (£115.2 million).
So the correct answer is (D) £198.1 million

4   Where's the information I need? Look in: *Conglomerate plc turnover by world region* and *Conglomerate plc projected UK regional sales (£ millions) for 2009.*
How do I calculate the answer?
The 2008 figure for the UK can be read directly from the table showing Conglomerate plc turnover by world region. This is £477.9 million
The 2009 figure is the sum of the projected UK regional sales figures, i.e. London total + Southern total + Northern total = 75.3 + 115.2 + 82.9 = 273.4
477.9 − 273.4 = 204.5
% difference = 100% × 204.5 / 477.9 = 43% (rounded up)
So the correct answer is (B) 43% decrease

5   Where's the information I need? Look in: *Conglomerate plc worldwide turnover by market sector* table.
How do I calculate the answer?
You need to calculate the difference in sales for each market sector between 2006 and 2008. This has already been done for question 2. The most profitable sector is Retail (£7.4 million increase in sales). The least profitable sector is Food markets (£19.3 million drop in sales)
Difference = 19.3 + 7.4 = £26.7 million
So the correct answer is (C) £26.7 million

6   Where's the information I need? Look in: *Product A, B, C sales in Year x* graph.
How do I calculate the answer?

Sales in Year x for Product A ($100,000s) = 23.6 + 33.7 +
45.3 + 29.5 + 42.2 = 174.3
174.3 (in $100,000s) = $17.4 million
Difference = $18 million − $17.4 million = $0.6 million
So the correct answer is (D) $0.6 million

7   Where's the information I need? Look in: *Product A, B, C
     sales in Year x* graph
     Calculate (in $100,000s to keep things simple) the total
     Product A, B and C sales for each world region shown:
     Asia-Pacific = 23.6 + 65.5 + 59.2 = 148.3
     North America = 33.7 + 24.8 + 34.6 = 93.1
     South America = 45.3 + 31.6 + 52 = 128.9
     Europe = 29.5 + 21.5 + 39 = 90
     Rest of World = 42.2 + 57.4 + 46.8 = 146.4
     The two regions with the lowest sales (Europe, North
     America) are those that when combined have sales less than
     $22 million ($9,000,000 + $9,300,000 = $18,300,000).
     So the correct answer is (C); Europe, North America

8   Where's the information I need? Look in: *Conglomerate plc
     operational source* table
     How do I calculate the answer?
     7.2 + 5.3 + 4.2 + 8.1 + 3.5 = $2.83 million
     So the correct answer is (C) $2.83 million

9   Where's the information I need? Look in: *Conglomerate plc
     operational source* table and *Total packaging sales* pie chart.
     Calculate the percentage of new business per region;
     Asia-Pacific = 100% × 7.2 / 42 = 17.1%
     North America = 100% × 4.2 / 85 = 4.9%
     South America = 100% × 8.1 / 18 = 45%
     Europe = 100% × 5.3 / 90 = 5.9%
     Rest of World = 100% × 3.5 / 20 = 17.5%
     So the correct answer is (D); South America

10   Where's the information I need? Look in: *Conglomerate plc total packaging sales* pie chart.
$90 : 20 = 9 : 2$
So the correct answer is (B); 9 : 2

11   Where's the information I need? Look in: *Conglomerate plc employees* table
Calculate the absolute change for each region by deducting the smallest from the largest number of employees (for the two years shown):
Asia-Pacific; $1,502 - 1,048 = 454$
Europe $= 6,453 - 6,375 = 78$
North America $= 2,406 - 2,392 = 14$
South America $= 1,558 - 1,415 = 143$
Rest of World $= 1,850 - 1,124 = 726$
So the correct answer is (C) Rest of World (greatest); North America (least)

12   Where's the information I need? Look in: *Conglomerate plc UK staff 2008* graph
Calculate graduate % within each function;
Corporate; $100\% \times 284 / 579 = 49.1\%$
Finance; $100\% \times 251 / 444 = 56.5\%$
Marketing; $100\% \times 182 / 317 = 57.4\%$
Engineering/IT; $100\% \times 259 / 714 = 36.3\%$
Operations; $100\% \times 178 / 476 = 37.4\%$
So the correct answer is (E) Marketing

13   Where's the information I need? Look in: *UK Conglomerate plc employee gender demographics* graph
Calculate the ratio for each year:
2004; $540 / 664 = 0.81$
2005; $605 / 844 = 0.72$
2006; $1,110 / 822 = 1.35$
2007; $1,480 / 930 = 1.59$
2008; $1,236 / 915 = 1.35$
So the correct answer is (B) 2006 and 2008

14   Where's the information I need? Look in: *2008 sales of 4 best selling food brands in UK* graph. Calculate the combined sales for each quarter:

	Quarter 1	Quarter 2	Quarter 3	Quarter 4
Deluxe and Extra Special	9 + 24 = 33	14 + 22 = 36	20 + 17 = 37	24 + 13 = 37
Supreme and Special	13 + 13 = 26	10 + 11 = 21	15 + 14 = 29	22 + 15 = 37

So the correct answer is (D) Quarter 4

15   Where's the information I need? Look in: *Retail sales for product a (£10,000s)* graph. Work out the differences, as follows:

	High street	Retail park	Difference
Jan	5.1	7.5	2.4
Feb	12.5	15	2.5
March	15.3	22.7	7.4
April	20.4	30.1	9.7
May	14.9	24.6	9.7
June	15.1	17.8	2.7
July	15.6	24.4	8.8
August	17.3	19.9	2.6

So the correct answer is (E) April, May

16   Where's the information I need? Look in: *2008 UK sales (in £ millions)* graph.
How do I calculate the answer?
Online figures can be read directly from the graph;
Deluxe = 25.4
Supreme = 23.2
Special = 24.4
Extra Special = 27.1. So Extra Special has the highest online sales
Online + Offline combined:
Deluxe = 58. So Deluxe has the highest overall (online and offline) sales

Supreme = 47

Special = 40

Extra Special = 52

**So the correct answer is (B) Extra Special (online);
Deluxe (overall)**

17 Where's the information I need? Look in: *Retail sales for
product a (£10,000s)* graph. The line graph for Retail park
sales is above the line graph for High Street retail sales for
each month shown.

So the correct answer is (A); None of these

18 Where's the information I need? Look in: *Retail sales for
product a (£10,000s)* graph. Review this to establish when
the line graph for Retail park sales and the line graph for
High Street retail sales are both sloping downwards.

So the correct answer is (C) April to May

19 Where's the information I need? Look in: *Conglomerate plc
staff costs* table.

Add up the total staff costs across 2006–8;

Salaries total = 4,477.5

Social security total = 541.9

Pension total = 509.6

Bonus payments total = 140.2

Misc. total = 528.6

So the correct answer is (B) Social security

20 You need to look in: *Conglomerate plc worldwide gross sales
turnover (to year end)* table to get the 2007 turnover figures.
Sum the 2007 turnover figures = 342.1 + 164.1 + 466 +
377.6 + 62.7 = 1,412.5 (£100,000s)

1 : 8 ratio so profit = turnover × 1 / 8 = 1,412.5 / 8 = 176.6
(£100,000s)

So the answer is (B) £177 million

21   For the Asian sales total look in the *Telecommunications company – non-UK sales* graph. For the UK sales total look in the *Telecommunications company – UK sales 2008 by market* graph.
Total UK sales = 82.8 (North) + 116.3 (South) + 74.4 (London) = £273.5 million
Total Asian sales = £150.6 million
Difference (to the nearest £ million) = £123 million
So the correct answer is (B) £123 million

22   Refer to the *Telecommunications company – non-UK sales* graph
Calculate the quarterly totals:
Quarter 1 = 132.5
Quarter 2 = 132.2
Quarter 3 = 123.8
Quarter 4 = 132.5
So the correct answer is (C) Quarter 1, Quarter 4

23   Refer to the *Telecommunications company – non-UK sales* graph
Add the relevant % increase to the relevant quarters:
Quarter 1: 132.5 × 103% = 136.48
Quarter 2: 132.2 × 104% = 137.49
Quarter 3: 123.8 × 105% = 129.99
Quarter 4: 132.5 × 106% = 140.45
Add up these totals = £544.41
So the correct answer is (A) £544.4 million

24   You need to look in: *Conglomerate plc UK functions* table.
Calculate the total costs for the 4 quarters;
Quarter 1 = 33.9
Quarter 2 = 35
Quarter 3 = 37.8
Quarter 4 = 36.8
Total = 143.5

Yearly budget = 142
Difference = 143.5 − 142 = 1.5 (in £100,000s) = £150,000
The correct answer is (E) £150,000

25 You need to look in: *Conglomerate plc UK functions* table. Calculate the differences between budget and cost for each function;
Sales/Marketing: 12 (budget) − 10.6 = 1.4
Production: 35 (budget) − 37.5 = −2.5
Operational: 64 (budget) − 65 = 1
Overheads: 7 (budget) − 6.6 = 0.4
Rent/office expenses: 24 (budget) − 23.8 = 0.2
So the correct answer is (B) Production

26 You need to look in: *Conglomerate plc worldwide turnover (to year end)* table and the *Conglomerate plc UK functions* table. Taking each statement at a time:
(A) Quarter 1 contributed the most to the budget over-spend.
FALSE − Calculate the totals for each quarter:
Quarter 1 = 33.9
Quarter 2 = 35
Quarter 3 = 37.8
Quarter 4 = 36.8
It is Quarter 3 where the most has been spent.
(B) Production has the highest yearly budget.
FALSE − Operations has the highest yearly budget
(C) Operational costs have been increasing between quarter 1 and quarter 4.
TRUE − You can see this visually from scanning the chart of figures. If you did this before going through some of the other statements (particularly statement (A) then well done you!)
(D) Worldwide turnover was highest in 2008.

FALSE – Worldwide turnover was highest in 2007

(E)Worldwide turnover for all three years was less than £4,100 million.

FALSE – Worldwide turnover = 1,380.2 + 1,412.5 + 1,396 = £4,188.7 million

So the correct answer is (C) Operational costs have been increasing between quarter 1 and quarter 4.

27 You need to look in: *Conglomerate plc worldwide turnover (to year end)* table.

Think through what the question is really asking. You can reinterpret the question as which had the highest sales worldwide. Hence you just need to total the sales for each:

Retail's total sales 2006–2008 = 1,022.9

Packaging's total sales 2006–2008 = 488.2

Food's total sales 2006–2008 = 1,375

Leisure's total sales 2006–2008 = 1,128.1

Other market's total sales 2006–2008 = 174.5

So the correct answer is (C) Food

28 Use the *Conglomerate plc employees by function* table's figures to work out each function's changes in staff numbers between 2006 and 2008:

Retail = 3,855 − 3,580 = 275 more employees

Logistics = 1,636 − 1,425 = 211 more employees

Packaging = 1,622 − 1,672 = 50 less employees

Food = 1,588 − 1,561 = 27 more employees

Leisure = 2,121 − 2,451 = 330 less empoyees

The question asks about the difference, so ignoring whether there has been more or less employees. The second largest difference is Retail.

So the correct answer is (A) Retail

29 Where's the information I need? Look in: the *Female packaging employees in 2008 (at Pennon location)* pie chart and the *Male packaging employees in 2008 (at Pennon location)* pie chart.

Calculate the ratio of male to female employees for each age band. I have simplified this by using a division for each, rather than going through the more laborious process of working out the ratio for each age band:

	Age <25	Age 25–29	Age 30–39	Age 40–49	Age 50–59
Female	132	166	217	55	25
Male	199	150	225	81	62
Ratio	199 / 132	150 / 166	225 / 217	81 / 55	62 / 25
	= 1.51	= 0.90	= 1.04	= 1.47	= 2.48

So the correct answer is (E) 50–59 years

brilliant tip

The ratio of male to female employees for those aged 50–59 years is far higher than for any of the other age bands. You could perhaps have got to this answer by writing down the respective numbers of male and female employees and then comparing them visually.

30 Where's the information I need? Look in: the *Female packaging employees in 2008 (at Pennon location)* pie chart and the *Male packaging employees in 2008 (at Pennon location)* pie chart

	age <25	age 25–29
Female	132	166
Male	199	150

So the correct answer is (C) 647

31 Look in: the *Conglomerate plc employees by function* table. This shows that the number of Retail employees in 2007 was 3,973.

Profits per employee = £79,460,000 / 3,973 = £20,000
So the correct answer is (B) £20,000

32   The *Conglomerate plc employees by function* table gives you the total number of Packaging employees in 2008 (1,622).
The male and female pie charts reveal the total number of employees at the Pennon site (607 females + 729 males = 1,336)
1,622 − 1,336 = 286 employees
So the correct answer is (B) 286

33   This range can be obtained by finding the largest gap between the two line graphs on the *Conglomerate plc share price (pence) against main competitor* graph. This gives you readings of 275p compared to 125p.
275 − 125 = 150
Thus the correct answer is (A) 0–150p

34   The *Predicted 2009 dividends per share* graph shows that the rivals have predicted dividends ranging from 20 pence to 35 pence. Conglomerate plc's predicted 2009 dividend is also shown as 30 pence. Hence to match each rival the dividend must rise by 5 pence to 35 pence.
$5/_{30} = 1/_6$
Thus the correct answer is (C) ⅙

35   Use the *Yield* graph to calculate the 2008 dividend = 175p × 2.75% = 4.81p
Read the 2009 Conglomerate plc dividend from the *Predicted 2009 dividends per share (pence)* graph = 30p.
Increase = 30 − 4.81 = 25.19
Thus the correct answer is (D) 25p

36   *The Conglomerate plc share price (pence) against main competitor* graph shows the average 2006 share price (£1.50).
Number of shares = 33,000 / 1.5 = 22,000
Thus the correct answer is (B) 22,000

37   The European subsidiary sales graph will give you the subsidiary that had the lowest sales in 2006 and the highest sales in 2007:
Thus the correct answer is (A) Subsidiary a (2006); Subsidiary e (2007)

38   Use the *Dividend (pence)* graph to calculate:
4,000 × 20p = 80,000p
Thus the correct answer is (B) £800

39   The highest point of the two line graphs in *Yield x shown (where dividend = x% of subsidiary share prices)* is the value of 4. This is for Subsidiary d and occurs in 2005.
Thus the correct answer is (D) 2005 (Subsidiary d)

40   Rather than calculating each percentage change in yield for Subsidiaries c and d look at the line graphs to see how possible each answer option is.

⭐ **brilliant** tip

This is an ideal question for working backwards from the answer options.

You need to match the following answer options . . .
(A)   2004–2005 (Subsidiary c)
(B)   2004–2005 (Subsidiary d)
(C)   2005–2006 (Subsidiary d)
(D)   2005–2006 (Subsidiary c)
(E)   2007–2008 (Subsidiary c)
. . . with where there has been the largest percentage as shown on the line graphs. Answer options A and D are clearly not the correct answer. That leaves B, C and E.
Between 2004 and 2005 Subsidiary d's yield changes by 100% from 2 to 4
Between 2005 and 2006 Subsidiary d's yield changes by 62.5% from 4 to 1.5

Between 2007 and 2008 Subsidiary c's yield changes by 33.3% from 1.5 to 2

Thus the correct answer is (B) 2004–2005 (Subsidiary d)

41 Use the *Conglomerate plc average graduate starting salary (in £)* graph to calculate the decrease in starting salary between 2007 and 2008:

24,500 − 24,000 = 500 decrease

Deduct this amount from the 2008 starting salary:

24,000 − 500 = 23,500

Thus the correct answer is (C) £23,500

42 Use the *Conglomerate plc average graduate starting salary (in £)* graph to calculate the average:

(23,000 + 22,500 + 24,000 + 24,500 + 24,000) / 5 = 23,600

Thus the correct answer is (D) £23,600

43 Calculate, using the *Average UK salary by function (2008)* table, the differences between Director and graduate salaries for each industry function:

Engineering/IT = 78.5 − 24.1 = 54.4

Operations = 74.8 − 23.6 = 51.2

Marketing = 75.4 − 22.4 = 53

Finance = 89.2 − 23.5 = 65.7

Corporate = 91.5 − 25.1 = 66.4

Thus the correct answer is (A) Corporate (greatest); Operations (least)

44 Referring to the *Average UK salary by function (2008)* table gives you the average Finance Director salary (£89,200). Convert this into Euros as follows:

89,200 × 1.12 = 99,904

Thus the correct answer is (D) 99,900 Euros

45 Use the *Length of service of graduate employees (2008)* pie

chart to find the percentage of graduate employees with a length of service less than 6 months (37% + 16% = 53%)

53% × 2,200 = 1,166

Thus the correct answer is (A) 1,166

46 Use the *Sales by region (£100,000s)* graph to establish that there are three possible periods when there has been a year-on-year decrease in regional sales:

Year 2 = 100% × (2,108 − 2,151) / 2,151 = 2% decrease

Year 3 = 100% × (1,725 − 2,108) / 2,108 = 18.2% decrease

Year 5 = 100% × (1,748 − 1,603) / 1,748 = 8.3% decrease

Thus the correct answer is (C) Year 3

47 Use the *European Quarter 1 – Retail chain performance* graph to calculate the overall sales:

Retail chain a total = 203.9

Retail chain b total = 181.9

Retail chain c total = 189.7

Retail chain d total = 225.5

Retail chain e total = 199.5

Thus the correct answer is (E) Retail chains d, a, e, c, b

48 Use the *Sales by region (£100,000s)* graph to calculate the total Asian sales across all five years:

765 + 727 + 605 + 611 + 545 = 3,253

Then convert from Euros:

3,253 × 1.11 = 3,610 (£100,000s)

Thus the correct answer is (A) €361 million

49 Use the *Sales by region (£100,000s)* graph to calculate the total North American earnings across all five years:

741 + 712 + 580 + 592 + 505 = 3,130 (£100,000s)

Thus the correct answer is (A) £313 million

Summary

So you've worked your way through the practice questions in Part 2 and are ready to tackle the actual test. Phew! Give yourself a pat on the back and take a well-deserved break. Well done for putting in the effort to practise. I know it might seem like a lot of work preparing for a test that lasts less than an hour, but it is time well spent when you consider the implications. A successful result takes you one step closer to realising your dreams and ambitions – be it a place on a training course, an exciting new job, or a lucrative promotion.

Let's recap for those readers who have completed plenty of practice and are feeling on top of things and then let's recap for other readers too. So, if you have completed the practice questions relevant to your upcoming test (and maybe many other practice questions too!) . . .

- You should be feeling much more confident about your numeracy skills.
- You will now know what to expect on your test day. This gives you a valuable advantage over the competition.
- You can refer back to Chapter 4 for some advice on mental preparation if you are concerned about dealing with nerves on the big day.
- You should relax and get a good night's sleep before the test.

If you feel that your maths skills are still a bit shaky I urge you to . . .

- Go back and attempt the practice questions again.

- Start with the easier chapters if you did not do this first time around.

- Pay closer attention to the answer explanations so you are clear on where you are going wrong.

- Each chapter in Part 2 also includes *Brilliant resources* boxes. Use these to access additional practice questions and find out as much as you can about your test.

- Try not to get discouraged if you are not improving as much as you'd like. Refreshing your numeracy skills takes time, especially if it has been a long time since you used them. If you practise enough, and learn from your mistakes, you will eventually see an improvement. It is important to stay positive.

It might not have been your intention when you picked up this book, but hopefully you have also benefited from improving your mental arithmetic skills. Rather than reaching for your calculator every time you need to do a simple mathematical operation, you might actually be able to save time by working out the answer in your head. It's a sure way to impress your friends when it comes to dividing up a restaurant bill!

Best of luck on your test day. I hope you perform to the best of your abilities and do yourself proud.